Sandra Mano

Instructor's Resource Manual

to accompany

American Mosaic
Multicultural Readings in Context
Third Edition

Barbara Roche Rico
Loyola Marymount University

Sandra Mano
University of California, Los Angeles

Houghton Mifflin Company   **Boston**   **New York**

Senior Sponsoring Editor: Suzanne Phelps Weir
Development Editor: Janet Young
Editorial Assistant: Kate Hartke
Associate Production/Design Coordinator: Lisa Jelly
Manufacturing Manager: Florence Cadran
Senior Marketing Manager: Nancy Lyman

Printed in the U.S.A.

ISBN: 0-395-88662-7

123456789–B+B–04 03 02 01 00

Contents

Preface

This guide presents suggestions for using *American Mosaic* effectively. Because we see both teaching and writing as processes that evolve from the rhetorical situation and involve the intentions of the teacher and writer, we offer suggestions rather than rules for procedure. We have also avoided. trying to provide answers to the questions that follow the readings since we see learning as a collaborative activity that should engage and center on students. Instead we encourage you to help students take responsibility for generating their own questions and answers. To this end, we have included the following features in our *Instructor's Resource Manual*.

With the increased multiethnic nature of the United States and the growing numbers of multicultural and multilingual students in our universities, teachers of composition have become even more aware of the need for readers that present writers who reflect the ethnic diversity of this country. Recently, authors and publishers have rushed to fill this gap with multiethnic readers. Most of these are thematic readers that deal with generic themes from a multicultural perspective. Our text differs from these because it presents particularly generative periods in the history of various ethnic groups in the United States and, after setting the context, lets the representative authors speak for themselves about issues of importance to them. We believe that all students will be enriched by hearing the voices of various ethnic writers and by understanding something about the periods in which they wrote and the contributions they made to this country. Students will also develop a fuller appreciation of the multicultural nature of contemporary American society.

This text presents the writing of most ethnic groups in the United States within a chronological framework. Each chapter reflects what we consider a significant period in the development of a particular ethnic group using readings that are representative of the attitudes and concerns of that period. Clearly, these people were writing before the period we selected and have continued writing since. Our intention is to suggest the richness of the American experience rather than provide a comprehensive coverage of American ethnic literature and history.

We chose to begin with readings that introduce various perspectives on some of the larger issues that the text covers. As a result selections in chapter 1 deals with topics such as assimilation versus accommodation, personal and cultural identity, immigration, and diversity. Chapter 2 introduces the writing of American Indians from an early speech by Chief Joseph to the present. Chapter 3 presents the writing of some of the many immigrant groups who flocked to the United States from Europe during the period of 1880–1910. Both of these groups share the general concerns and introduce themes that reappear in the chapters that follow: achieving success, coping with discrimination, loss of culture and identity, and generational conflicts.

Chapters 4 through 8 focus on specific ethnic groups. In some chapters, the readings are from a brief and particularly generative period, such as the years of the Japanese internment. In others, such as chapter 6 on the Puerto Rican writers, the readings span several years. The difference in focus resulted from several factors, including availability, quality, and relevance of the material.

Chapter 4 focuses on the Chinese immigrants who came to the West Coast in the late 1880s. Chapter 5 combines some material from our previous chapter on the Harlem Renaissance and material on the civil rights movement. Chapter 6 surveys the writing of Puerto Ricans in New York. Chapter 7 presents the often-neglected experience of the Japanese Americans during World War II from their own perspective. Chapter 8 introduces the works of Chicano writers.

Chapter 9, like chapter 1, presents representative voices from several groups. Some speak of the experiences of the many new immigrants to the United States. Others, longtime Americans, reflect on their own personal and cultural histories.

Each chapter begins with an introduction that presents major historical events and conditions of the period that shaped the group or groups represented. This helps students understand the context of the readings. The introduction ends with a section on literary voices that acquaints students with the writers and readings in the chapter. A photo essay at the beginning of each chapter further helps students visualize the historical context. The readings begin with an important historical document that reflects the key issues faced by the group represented. Following that are the selections—short stories, poems, or essays—by authors from the group. Each chapter ends with a contemporary essay that reflects on the issues raised in the chapter from a modern perspective.

Each chapter contains pre-reading, discussion/writing, and connecting questions designed to engage students in the readings, encourage them to read closely, and help them make connections among pieces within chapters and throughout the book.

A Beginning: Pre-reading/Writing activity follows the introduction to the chapter. This exercise aims to get students to think about some aspect of the experiences reported in the chapter before they read the material. This activity generates interest in the topic and encourages students to recall what they already know about the topic; students who are members of the group represented in the chapter can share their expertise. We've designed the pre-reading activity to last approximately one class period. Each pre-reading activity and all of the questions will be discussed in part 2 of this manual.

Following each selection are three or four Responding questions. The first question suggests a journal or short in-class writing assignment that often tries to help students relate the material in the reading to their personal experience and knowledge. It is especially important for all students to share experiences when dealing with multicultural readings. Students who are members of a particular ethnic group can share their expertise. Students who are not members of that group can recognize the shared human experience that cuts across ethnic and cultural boundaries. The second question presents an opportunity for collaborative learning as it sets up small group assignments. Though the tasks can be carried out individually, they are designed to help students share knowledge and have the opportunity to participate in a small-group discussion. The teacher and the text are then no longer the only sources of knowledge. The last two questions suggest specific essay topics. Question three usually asks students to write an essay based on close reading. Sometimes this question requires a restatement of the author's main points. Question four also asks students to write an essay, but the topic of the essay is broader in scope and often asks students to analyze the relationship between the ideas in the reading and a variety of other contexts.

The questions generally are designed to promote close reading of the text and encourage discussion and writing. Some specifically call for students to discuss or to write, but all can be adapted to either mode. The questions prompt a range of responses from the personal to the scholarly. Most likely you will not want to use all of the questions; rather you and your students can select whichever questions fit your own interests or classroom situations.

Each chapter ends with an extensive list of Connecting questions. The Connecting questions begin by asking students to connect readings within the chapter and then move on to help them make connections with other chapters. These are designed to promote analytical thinking about the selections and to help students connect ideas, themes, and issues throughout the text. You may find the thematic table of contents in part 3 of this manual helpful in approaching these questions.

The Connecting questions are broader and more complex than the Responding questions that follow each reading. They highlight the similarity of experiences among different ethnic and cultural groups and point up connections to other readings in the text whenever possible. Your students may choose to answer just one question, or individual students may choose different questions and share their answers with the class. We believe students should be given the opportunity to respond to questions that interest them or to create their own questions. Several of the questions give students the option to design their own essay topic; this approach often engages students more closely and produces livelier essays.

Each set of Connecting questions contains some questions entitled "For Further Research." These are intended for classes that include research papers as part of the curriculum. The topics require extensive outside reading.

Before we begin with specifics on how to use this book, we need to say a word about names and naming. One problem in creating a multicultural reading text is the use of names of ethnic groups that may be in the process of changing. We have tried as much as possible to refer to groups by the names they themselves used at particular periods in history. The issue of naming is a controversial one and would be an interesting topic for class discussion.

S. M.

New "Theme(s) for English B":
Reimagining Contexts for Learning in Multiethnic Writing Classes

Introduction

In his poem "Theme for English B," Langston Hughes writes:

> It's not easy to know what is true for you or me
> at twenty two, my age. But I guess I'm what
> I feel and see and hear, Harlem, I hear you:
> hear you, hear me—we too—you, me, talk on this page.

Hughes' poem addresses the Harlem of the 1920s; yet in many ways, in the Los Angeles and other urban centers of the 1990s, in classrooms across the country. Hughes' questions are still our questions: How do we manage the conversation of the classroom? Who enters the conversation when our students and we "talk on this page"? As writing professionals we have spent much of the last decade debating questions related to pluralism and the canons of our curricula. Those of us who teach courses with a multiethnic focus have devised our own response to the challenges voiced by E. D. Hirsch and Allan Bloom. Few of us would be teaching this material if we truly found that pluralism led us or our students down the slippery slope to cultural illiteracy, or if we believed that to open the canon meant to close one's mind. Many of us would agree with Gadamer that the meaning of a given text resides in the historical place of the interpreter; or with M. M. Bakhtin, who suggests that to endow any object or artifact with aesthetic value is a social act, inseparable from prevailing ideologies. We see in the early anthologies of American literature a tendency to celebrate the nativism of Longfellow over the less accessible poems of Dickinson and Whitman. The pattern can be seen as well with schools of criticism: the New Critics, who valued such features as wit and paradox, helped to strengthen the critical reputation of Donne; the formalists, who stressed the importance of defamiliarization, turned to Sterne's *Tristram Shandy*; the structuralists found inspiration in British romantic poetry and Baudelaire. As the work of Barbara Herrnstein Smith and John Guillory has shown, literary values that are at one moment called "universal" are in essence contingent upon social values, socially constructed systems of belief.

There is no need to reenact the debates of the last decade. It is not so much that these debates have been settled, but scholars have more or less chosen sides and moved on. Questions are being redefined from whether to how. Those of us who have chosen to listen more to the voices of our

John Alberti, ed., *The Canon in the Classroom: The Pedagogical Implications of Canon Revision in America.* Copyright © 1995 by Garland Publishing. Reprinted with permission.

own students than the caveats of those critics opposed to curricular change have found in multi-ethnic approaches some new opportunities for intellectual growth, both as teachers and as learners. But after ten years of developing multicultural textbooks and multiethnic courses, we are left to ask, How much has really changed? How much have we been changed by the "broadening of the literary canon"? By making our classes more "multicultural" by including new authors, have we really begun to create an environment in which our students will feel more comfortable to speak their truths in the classroom, and to "talk" to us on the page? Or have we just allowed ourselves to become a little more comfortable?

We might assert that the greatest threat to the development of multiethnic courses, or multiethnic approaches to writing, is not the criticisms of the conservatives, but the complacency of the converted. To see this, we would like to examine a few of the ways in which traditional literature and writing courses have been modified in the last decade to reflect a multicultural perspective.

Thematic Approaches

In the 1980s critics such as Walter Ong, Raymund Paredes, and others proposed the use of multi-ethnic works in what Ong referred to as "interactive organization." Canonical systems could be put into dialogic relationship to help illuminate thematic correspondences. We have adopted such interactive approaches in our own classrooms, and we have found that they can introduce a new perspective to themes common to the freshman English class: ambitions and responsibilities, the struggle for identity, the search for selfhood, and the attraction and delusion of the American dream. The critique of the American dream, which finds its expression in so much American fiction and drama of the 1940s and 1950s, takes on a new sense of urgency in the literature of historically marginalized groups. Useful discussions have resulted from pairings of Tennessee Williams' *Glass Menagerie* with Sandra Cisneros' short novel *The House on Mango Street*, which treats the life of a young woman growing up in Chicago. In both works there is a strong sense of the individual's alienation from and isolation in the urban landscape, the young person's striving for a better life beyond that of the crowded apartment.

Moreover, the sense of struggle for one's goal despite the opinions of the larger society, which emerges clearly in Eudora Welty's "A Worn Path," is expressed in an interesting way in Thomas Rivera's story "La Noche buena." Rivera's story follows the journey of a woman—the wife of a migrant worker—as she seeks to buy presents for her children on Christmas Eve. Here, too, we can sense the derision that she faces as she tries to negotiate her way through the town, the suspicion of the townspeople, and her resolution not to come home empty-handed.

The issues of familial and cultural tensions, the child's sense of responsibility, and his desire for self-respect emerge quite pointedly in a discussion that includes Faulkner's "Barn Burning" and Richard Wright's "The Man Who Was Almost a Man." The dialogic organization of texts has much to recommend it. It prompts students to explore values from a comparative perspective. As Elizabeth Fox-Genovese has suggested, canonical works help to articulate the values of the society that has produced them. As Ong has pointed out, the interaction of works from dominant and marginalized sectors of society can encourage students to explore works and cultural values from new perspectives:

> A minority literature often mixes what is unfamiliar with the majority with what is familiar. It thus provides not only an organization of experience different from that of the majority culture (and of other minorities), but also an interactive organization. A minority literature often negotiates for its own identity with the majority culture and constantly redefines itself, ultimately bringing the majority culture to redefine itself more adequately, too. (3)

This organization can enable students to see "creative tensions" among works. Speaking about Chicano literature's relation to the dominant culture, Ramon Saldívar has asserted:

As a part of American literature, narratives by Chicano men and women offer significant representations of the historical drama of nineteenth and twentieth century American life, especially as that
life intersects, consciously or not, with what has sometimes been referred to as the Third World. (24)

Explorations of marginalized literature can encourage students to develop new ways of evaluating
the literary production of both the marginalized and the dominant cultures. Works from each
culture can be seen to problematize the value system of the other.

For an interactive organization to be effective, however, there must be a diligent attention to
issues of emphasis, perspective, and balance. Imagine, for example, a class discussion exploring
three texts with female protagonists: the traditional Griselda story (recounted in Chaucer's
"Clark's Tale"), Maxine Hong Kingston's *Woman Warrior,* and Alice Walker's *Color Purple.* The
interactive organization would seem to provide an interesting groundwork for exploring, for example, issues related to gender and class in all three works. We might ask our students to consider
how these issues can affect a character's sense of self-determination, or how familial control and
more public power structures are related to each other in each text. Such an examination might be
fruitful, so long as appropriate attention were paid to the unique voice of each literary work.

This is where issues of perspective and emphasis come in. Without a concerted effort to treat
each work on its own terms, an interactive organization might tend to privilege the more established, more canonical work—making the Griselda story the central subtext, while representing
Walker's or Hong Kingston's narratives as other versions of that story. In such an organization,
the less canonical works can be co-opted to highlight newer elements of the dominant-culture
work. What emerges is less a conversation among works than a chiaroscuro (to use an admittedly
Eurocentric term) in which the values of the other works are determined by their power to set off
the more canonical one. In such a formulation, those elements present in Hong Kingston or Walker
but absent from the traditional story will be overlooked.

Many anthologies that present themselves as being multicultural illustrate another problem
with the thematic approach. Too often the thematic structure is not really interactive at all.
Many introductory literature and composition readers, for example, offer dialogic pairings less
often than a thematically arranged list of titles—often the same handful of authors, the same
"critical war-horses" replicated in each anthology. A few examples will help to make the point:
Maya Angelou's "Graduation," Ellison's "Battle Royal," Wakatsuki's "Arrival at Manzanar,"
Rodriguez's "New American Scholarship Boy," the first chapter from Hong Kingston's *Woman
Warrior,* and Martin Luther King's "I Have a Dream" speech. Our intention is less to comment on
the works themselves, but to explore some of the ways in which their inclusion—indeed, their
ubiquity—in introductory literature and writing collections can prompt students to have a simplis-
tic, perhaps even monologic sense about the issues involved.

In terms of this rather limited "rhetoric of inclusion," we note the presence of the early
Richard Rodriguez and, more recently, the emergence of Dinesh D'Souza. The formal elegance of
Rodriguez's prose has been noted by many; one wonders whether the reprinting of "New American
Scholarship Boy" might be related to the ways in which Rodriguez's rhetoric can be seen to
reflect positions valorized by the neoconservative movement. Similarly D'Souza becomes the
"ethnic" representative that decries the multicultural trends as "illiberal education." As impor-
tant as what is included is what is left out: we see much less often the writings of John Okada,
Gloria Anzaldúa, or until recently, Malcolm X.

Often what tends to be emphasized by thematic organization and the selection of choices is
unity rather than diversity, harmony rather than tension. Such approaches tend to encourage
ahistorical readings that overlook or deny the importance of cultural difference. This can prompt
students to feel that having read the work of one writer from a representative group will allow
them to make general statements about others. Having read Rodriguez, they can generalize about
affirmative action or the dangers of bilingualism; having read Hong Kingston, they know how
Chinese American women feel about keeping silent. One might be tempted to use Hirsch's phrase
in describing this approach as "piecemeal undigested knowledge"—incomplete and devoid of
context.

When anthologies do include material focusing on prejudice or inequality, these works are often approached from a safe, and thus nonthreatening, position of historical distance. By reprinting Maya Angelou's "Graduation" or Ellison's "Battle Royal," are we allowing our students to conclude that they are encountering rarefied artifacts from another time, and to assume that the problems encountered by the narrator are not their problems, or the problems of students today? Do we teach these works as on the other side of the *Brown* v. *Board* decision or the civil rights movement? Do we let them assert that the problems depicted in those stories don't exist anymore? The events of April 1992 in Los Angeles and other urban cities have clearly eliminated this "comfort zone," if it ever indeed existed.

Contextual Approaches

Hughes' poem invites us to acknowledge the importance of context: to listen to the individual, the history, the collective memory, that "talks on this page." To recognize the importance of context is to be aware of the culture that speaks through the writer, that enables him or her to speak; it is also to recognize those elements that keep the student from talking. In our enthusiasm for multiculturalism, we cannot allow our explorations of multiethnic cultures to become self-generating, self-congratulatory retreats. We cannot isolate our examinations of cultural expression from the polarized, balkanized contexts in which we find ourselves living. What "talks on the page" is not only life story, but the controversies of immigration, bilingualism, affirmative action, and racism.

An approach to multiethnic texts that introduces and recognizes the importance of context can draw the interpreter away from a work as an isolated artifact and towards the work as a part of a more complex cultural moment. This includes a consideration of the circumstances of its production and its reception. It raises questions about the audience for that text and the authority that it assumes for itself in relationship with other literary texts and cultural markers. Context means acknowledging difference, uniqueness; as Hughes writes "Will my page be colored that I write? Being me, it will not be white."

To chose a contextual approach rather than a strictly thematic one is to acknowledge the possibility of difference, of uniqueness. Rather than present a multicultural menu on the general theme of insider or outsider, one might enter into the literature of an ethnic group, isolate particularly generative periods in the history of the group. What prompted literary texts to be produced? What sort of texts were produced? In what sense did they relate to each other? What images dominate? How are they transformed? What is the relationship between the author and other authors? In what ways does the culture "talk" on the page? What is the history of the work's reception? How is it received today? One example of how this might work would be an examination of the Internment as history, memory, and image in Japanese-American literature. The issuing of the Evacuation Order caused individuals both within and outside the Japanese-American community to reconsider the meaning of American constitutional guarantees. As Monica Sone and others have described, both citizen and noncitizen residents had to question whether nationality, national origin, or ethnicity would take precedence over constitutional guarantees.

Much of Japanese-American literature written both during and after the Internment reflects, reflects on, and represents the situation of being "in camp"—what it was like to be deprived of one's land and forced to live under regimented conditions, imprisoned without trial. Marginalized, forced to retire from the commerce and community they had known, detainees were left with little but time—time to consider their circumstances, time to write. There emerged a microcosm that contained not only schools but also newspapers, journals, and literary societies, whose authors and audience were "in camp." A generation used the language of confinement to call attention to its own circumstances and to consider the consequences of that confinement on issues related to identity, affiliation, and belonging.

The Internment provides both an important historical moment and a governing image in much Japanese-American literature, even that written years after the camps had been closed. To explore Japanese-American texts from the perspective of the camps is to establish a context in which a set of texts is allowed to speak, not as the isolated representation of a single ethnic group, but as a part of a particularly generative period of literary production. Themes such as identity and loyalty that are represented in Japanese-American texts become more problematic when viewed in terms of the historical context that helped to shape them: Toshio Mori's short stories which had been accepted for publication just before the War, only to be rejected right after Pearl Harbor, or John Okada's *No-no Boy,* a novel about an internee who refused to serve in the military, written by a man who was himself an internee and a decorated veteran of World War II. These themes, historically grounded in the Japanese-American experience, reemerge in the works of other writers, among them Hisaye Yamamoto. Much of Yamamoto's short fiction (published in popular magazines during the 1950s and 60s, but not collected in book form until the late 1980s) explores the ways in which life in the camp helps to define and dictate the sort of life one would have in the future. "Las Vegas Charley," for example, explores consequences of the internment, the ways in which one character's life continues to be shaped by the political choices made years before. "The Legend of Miss Sasagawara" presents a young woman's coming of age as a person and a writer within the confines of the camp experience.

As the poetry of Lawson Fusao Inada and Janice Mirikitani illustrates, the camp image can sometimes be fused with other historical references to create a more general statement about subjugation and silencing. In Inada's poem "Concentration Constellation," the western landscape is presented as a constellation, each point of which marks the site of an internment camp:

> Begin between the Golden State's
> highest and lowest elevations
> and name that location
>
> Manzanar. Rattlesnake a line
> southward to the zone
> of Arizona, to the home
> of Natives on the reservation
> and call those Gila, Poston . . .
>
> Now regard what sort of shape
> this constellation takes
> It sits there like a jagged scar,
> massive, on the massive landscape.
> It lies there like the rusted wire
> of a twisted and remembered fence.

In the poem the camp image overtakes the geography of the continent, so that the entire southwest is seen in relation to the "constellation" of camps. In the image of Poston, one kind of detention fuses with another as the poet makes note of the reservations built to contain Native American Indians. In Mirikitani's more often quoted "We the Dangerous," the allusions to the Internment coexist alongside allusions to other moments of conquest, subjugation, and annihilation:

> We the dangerous
> Dwelling in the ocean.
> Akin to the jungle.
> Close to the earth.
>
> Hiroshima.
> Vietnam.
> Tule Lake.
>
> And yet we are not devoured.
> And yet we are not humbled.
> And yet we are not broken.

If Mirikitani's poem asserts a kind of cultural strength—a refusal to be "broken"—many of the other works produced in response to the Internment articulate a refusal to be silenced. In fiction and nonfiction, essays and historical accounts, writers such as David Mura, Garrett Hongo, and Ronald Takaki are asserting the importance of "overcoming the silence" that has marked the community's response to the Internment. Garrett Hongo's essay "Kubota," for example, examines the reciprocal nature of the debts each generation owes to the other: to tell the stories. In his chapters treating the Internment in *Strangers from a Different Shore,* Ronald Takaki shows the importance of telling the history from the perspective of an insider.

This approach allows issues to emerge that are important to a particular group. Thus, rather than having a conventional list of "universal themes" imposed from the outside, the class discussion is grounded in themes that have emerged from the historical and cultural experience of the groups. From this perspective, the class can then examine issues such as property, entitlement, loyalty, and responsibilities in a more informed manner. It also provides a new context for more fully examining the issues of competition, resentment, and stereotyping based on race, which seem to have reemerged in some sectors of business and academia. Historical and cultural context helps to inform and ground these discussions.

Just as the Internment has had an effect on the Japanese-American community that has continued long after the closing of the camps, the border has become a significant, recurring image in the writings of Chicanos. While some of our students may feel secure in their assumptions that the border is established and needs only to be protected with greater resolve, much of the history and literature of Chicanos problematizes the issue of the border and, with it, issues related to ownership, entitlement, loyalty, and identity. Indeed, from the signing of the Treaty of Guadalupe Hidalgo in 1848, in which Mexico ceded much of its land to the United States, the issue of border crossing has been a pervasive theme in Chicano literature.

An exploration of Chicano literature from a contextual perspective might involve an examination of the border as a legal, historical, and metaphorical construct in Chicano narratives from the signing of the treaty to the present, or it might focus on the writings that helped to shape the "Chicano movement," from the mid 1960s, when the concerns of the farm workers movement helped to bring to the forefront again issues related to the legal and economic status of those who had crossed the border to find employment.

Gloria Anzaldúa's mixed-mode essay *Borderlands/La Frontera* calls the border "una hedira abierta where the Third World grates against the first and bleeds" (193). In presenting another history of immigration (which notes the illegal immigration to Mexican territory in the 1800s), another view of the Alamo ("the symbol that legitimized the white imperialist takeover"), Anzaldúa offers another way of contextualizing the border culture:

> We have a tradition of migration, a tradition of long walks. Today we are witnessing *la migración de los pueblos mexicanos,* the return odyssey to the historical/mythological Aztlán. This time the traffic is from south to north.
>
> *El retorno* to the promised land first began with the Indians from the interior of Mexico and the *mestizos* that came with the *conquistadores* in the 1500s. Immigration continued in the next three centuries, and in this century, it continued with the *braceros* who helped to build our railroads and who picked our fruit. Today thousands of Mexicans are crossing the border legally and illegally; ten million people without documents have returned to the Southwest. (11, emphases hers)

In Anzaldúa's formulation, the crossing of borders in which the migrants are engaged is less a violation of law than a return to the homeland. The border is not absolute but shifting; like other metaphors, its mobility can serve a multitude of perceptual or rhetorical objectives.

As Anzaldúa suggests elsewhere, the border as a formulation is relevant, not only for the newer immigrant but for anyone who is, as Pat Mora suggests, "bilingual and bicultural." Much of the work of more recent Chicano writers has focused on the intersection of border issues with other issues of affiliation and entitlement. An early chapter of Arturo Islas's *Migrant Souls,* for example, employs irony when describing the family's crossing the border back to Mexico in order to obtain a turkey for their "American style" Thanksgiving celebration. The drive down to the border prompts a discussion of names and their implications:

> On the way to the bridge, Josie made the mistake of asking her father if they were aliens. Sancho put his foot on the brake so hard that Eduviges almost rear-ended the truck. He looked at Josie very hard and said, "I do not ever want to hear you use that word in my presence again. About anybody. We are American citizens of Mexican heritage. We are proud of both countries and have never and will never be that word you just said to me."

When the father is reminded that the newspapers and one of the European-American school children use that word, he responds:

> "The next time she tells you that, you tell her that Mexican and Indian people were in this part of the country long before any gringos, Europeans (he said Yurrop-beans) or anyone else decided it was theirs . . ." She watched him look straight ahead, then in the rearview mirror, then at Josie.
>
> "Don't you see, Josie? When people calls Mexicans those words it makes it easier for them to deport or kill them. Aliens come from outer space . . . Sort of like your mother's family, the blessed Angels, who think they come from heaven. Don't tell her I said that."

Before he made that last comment, Josie was impressed by her father's tone. Sancho seldom became that passionate in their presence about any issue. He laughed at the serious and the pompous, especially religious fanatics. Here the ironic mode—the distance between the narrative voice and that of the father—prevents the father's words from becoming a diatribe. The issues of identity, loyalty, and respect are brought up by a father to his children who wished they had not raised the subject in the first place; the use of "Yurropbeans" adds to both the realism and the irony of the scene, without fully negating what is being asserted. The narrative, which monitors the father's actions (looking forward toward the border and back toward his wife following in the car behind) reinforces the connections between geographical and legal borders and the social borders created by language. Other works extend their examinations of the borders to consider issues of language, class, and gender. Pat Mora's poem "Legal Alien," for example, ponders the ways in which the choice or use of language can be read as affiliation:

> Bi-lingual, Bi-cultural,
> able to slip from "How's life?"
> to "Me'stan volviendo loca,"
> able to sit in a paneled office
> drafting memos in smooth English,
> able to order in fluent Spanish
> at a Mexican restaurant,
> American but hyphenated,
> viewed by Anglos as perhaps exotic,
> perhaps inferior, definitely different,
> viewed by Mexicans as alien.

Like many other Chicana and Chicano poets from Miguel Mendez on, Mora breaks a boundary of convention by having the Spanish and the English coexist in the same poem. In this poem, however, the linguistic coexistence only underlines the dualism about which the poem speaks. While the surface of the poem repeatedly asserts "I am able," the Spanish sentence becomes an acknowledgment of the burden attached to the bicultural, hyphenated existence.

The examples mentioned above show alternatives to the more conventional, thematic approaches of the past. Critical authority is constituted by one's responsiveness not only to a set of generalized issues, externally imposed onto the text, regardless of its culture. Instead, the thematic considerations are reformulated in response to the historical ones. In this way, the lived experience and earlier forms of cultural production provide a context for what follows. The works of a given author not only assert their difference in terms of their dominant culture; they can also "talk" to each other on the page.

Authority, Marginality, and the Mosaic

The richness of a work can be fairly appraised or fully appreciated only when one has made himself or herself familiar with the context itself in historical, political, or social terms. For those of us from the dominant culture, learning to teach multiethnic literature in a thoughtful way, one must become a student of multiethnic literature. One must exchange a position of relative security for one of risk; one must give up some of one's authority in order to become credible. Barbara Johnson describes this process in her essay on Zora Neale Hurston:

> One of the presuppositions with which I began was that Hurston was situated "outside" the mainstream literary canon and that I, by implication, was an institutional "insider." I soon came to see, however, not only that the insider becomes an outsider the minute she steps out of the inside, but also Hurston's work itself was constantly dramatizing and undercutting just such inside/outside oppositions, transforming the plane geometry of physical space into the complex transactions of discursive exchange. In other words, Hurston could be read not just as an example of the "noncanonical" writer, but as a commentator on the dynamics of any encounter between an inside and an outside, any attempt to make a statement about difference. (172–73)

It is important for those of us teaching the literature of the marginalized to experience in some sense the discomfort that accompanies marginality. Acknowledging this position of vulnerability is essential if one seeks to establish credibility and authority in the classroom. And as Freire and others have suggested, the authority that emerges should be of a new kind, less dependent on hierarchies, more reliant on shared expertise.

One cannot acknowledge one's marginality vis-à-vis a tradition in one moment and then return to the position of critical or generic gatekeeper the next. Many of us would be unwilling to label Cisneros' *Woman Hollering Creek* uneven, for example, lest we seem to be assigning primarily New Critical standards, to be privileging evenness, balance, organic unity as universal values. Yet many who would be reluctant to employ such criteria routinely insist on limiting their choice in introductory writing classes to those works—multiethnic or not—that illustrate and employ the conventions of the analytical essay, the deductive argument; for the perception remains that it is these texts, and not the "more literary ones," that will teach our students how to think critically and how to write. It is our view that to assert this position does justice to neither the works themselves nor the talents of our students. The introduction of multiethnic works into the composition classroom has been challenged by Werner Sollors and others as being incomplete without acknowledging its own incompleteness. In his 1986 essay, "A Critique of Pure Pluralism," for example, Sollors asserts:

> The dominant assumption among serious scholars who study ethnic literary history seems to be that history can best be written by separating the groups that produced such literature in the United States. The published results of this "mosaic" procedure are the readers and compendiums made up of diverse essays on groups of writers who may have little in common except so-called ethnic roots while, at the same time, obvious and important literary and cultural connections are obfuscated. (255)

While deprecating "so-called ethnic roots," Sollors is describing a construct that privileges intracultural factors while devaluing cross-cultural ones. One must acknowledge that any process of categorization is incomplete and to some degree subjective. It remains to be asked, however, whether what Sollors is describing is less a mosaic than an interpretive tunnel. For at the heart of the mosaic is an evershifting relationship between part and whole: the parts comprise the whole, but the meaning of each part is informed by its relationship to the whole. One's perception of the mosaic depends upon one's perspective—the position of the reader, audience, interpreter. Meaning is thus not so much discovered as socially constructed. The responsibility for interpretation is not appropriated by an authority figure, but is retained by the students themselves. As interpreters of cultural artifacts, students of the mosaic are not kept at a distance, but are invited in. In contrast to the silent reverential approach of the chiaroscuro, the mosaic approach allows students to establish their own boundaries and assert their own interpretive voices.

Works Cited

Anzaldúa, Gloria. *Borderlands/La Frontera: The New Mextiza.* San Francisco: Spinsters—Aunt Lute, 1987.

———. "The Homeland, Aztlán/El Otro Mexico." *Aztlán: Essays on the Chicano Homeland.* Eds. Rudolfo Anaya and Francisco Lomelí. Albuquerque: U of New Mexico P, 1989. 191–204.

Bercovitch, Sacvan, ed. *Reconstructing American Literary History.* Cambridge: Harvard UP, 1981.

Bloom, Allan. *The Closing of the American Mind.* NY: Simon and Schuster, 1987.

Calderon, Hector, and José David Saldívar, eds. *Criticism in the Borderlands: Studies in Chicano Literature, Culture, and Ideology.* Durham: Duke UP, 1990.

Chin, Frank. "Come All Ye Asian American Writers of the Real and the Fake." *The Big AIIIEEEEE! An Anthology of Chinese American and Japanese American Literature.* Eds. Frank Chin et al. NY: Meridian, 1991. 1–93.

Crawford, John F. "Notes toward a Multicultural Criticism: Three Works by Women of Color." *Gift of Tongues: Challenges in Contemporary American Poetry.* Eds. Marie Harris and Kathleen Aguero. Athens: U of Georgia P. 155–95.

Dickstein, Morris. "Popular Fiction and Critical Values: The Novel as a Challenge to Literary History." *Reconstructing American Literary History.* Ed. Sacvan Bercovitch. Cambridge: Harvard UP, 1981. 29–66.

Fox-Genovese, Elizabeth. "The Claims of Common Culture: Race, Class, and the Canon." *Salmagundi* 72 (1986): 131–43.

Gates, Henry Louis, Jr. *Black Literature and Literary Theory.* NY: Methuen, 1984.

———. "Pluralism and its Discontents." *Profession* 92 (1992): 35–38.

———. *Loose Canons.* NY: Oxford UP, 1992.

Graff, Gerald. *Professing Literature: An Institutional History.* Chicago: U of Chicago P, 1987.

Guillory, John. "Canonical and Non-canonical: A Critique of the Current Debate." *ELH* 54 (1987): 483–527.

Hirsch, E. D., Jr. *Cultural Literacy.* Boston: Houghton Mifflin, 1987.

Inada, Lawson Fusao. *Before the War: Poems as They Happened.* NY: Morrow, 1971.

———. "Of Place and Displacement: The Range of Japanese American Literature." *Three American Literatures: Essays on Chicano, Native American, and Asian Literature for Teachers of American Literature.* Ed. Houston Baker, Jr. NY: MLA, 1982. 54–65.

Islas, Arturo. *Migrant Souls.* NY: Morrow, 1990.

Jameson, Fredric. *The Political Unconscious.* Ithaca: Cornell UP, 1981.

Johnson, Barbara. *A World of Difference.* Baltimore: Johns Hopkins UP, 1989.

Kafka, Phillipa. "Multicultural Introduction to Literature." *Practicing Theory in Introductory College Literature Courses.* Eds. James M. Cahalan and David B. Downing. Urbana: NCTE, 1991. 179–88.

Kim, Elaine. *Asian American Literature.* Philadelphia: Temple UP, 1980.

Krupat, Arnold. *The Voice in the Margin: Native American Literature and the Canon.* Berkeley: U of California P, 1989.

Lauter, Paul. *Canons and Contexts.* NY: Oxford UP, 1990.

Lim, Shirley Geok-lin. "Twelve Asian American Writers in Search of Self-Definition." *Redefining American Literary History.* Eds. A. LaVonne Brown Ruoff and Jerry W. Ward, Jr. NY: MLA, 1990. 237–50.

Mirikitani, Janice. *Awake in the River.* San Francisco: Isthmus, 1978.

Mora, Pat. *Chants.* Houston: Arte Publico, 1984.

Ong, Walter J. "Introduction: On Saying We and Us to Literature." *Three American Literatures: Essays on Chicano, Native American, and Asian Literature for Teachers of American Literature.* Ed. Houston Baker, Jr. NY: MLA, 1982. 3–7.

Paredes, Raymund. "The Evolution of Chicano Literature." *Three American Literatures: Essays on Chicano, Native American, and Asian Literature for Teachers of American Literature.* Ed. Houston Baker, Jr. NY: MLA, 1982. 33–79.

Perkins, David. *Theoretical Issues in Literary History.* Cambridge: Harvard UP, 1990.

Said, Edward. *The World, the Text, and the Critic.* Cambridge: Harvard UP, 1983.

Sollors, Werner. "A Critique of Pure Pluralism." *Reconstructing American Literary History.* Ed. Sacuan Bereovitch. Cambridge: Harvard UP, 1986. 250–279.

PART I
SUGGESTIONS FOR USING AMERICAN MOSAIC

We have designed this text to be used with process pedagogy. We assume that students will have a voice in deciding on essay topics and that these essays will go through a series of drafts that will be reviewed by both peers and the instructor. We believe the book is adaptable to the most liberatory and student-centered workshop approach. However, it is also adaptable to the traditional classroom. We want to describe briefly several possible ways of organizing a course using this text. Considerations of time, your personality and inclination, and your students' interests and needs will determine which format you choose.

Course Organization

We recommend that you create a writing workshop in your classroom. In such a class, the focus is on students as readers and writers and the goal is to make the classroom into a community of writers. To achieve this end, you will need to involve students in both individual and collaborative activities centering around pre-writing, composing, and editing.

You have several options for organizing your class. Activities can be designed and initiated by you and/or your students. Whole-class discussions can be led by you or groups of students as long as the emphasis is on reading and writing as a process with less weight placed on final products and more on the process used to arrive at them. Papers are always in process and are always being revised. In such courses comments (either oral or written) rather than grades are the response to drafts. Sometimes final drafts are graded throughout the course, but sometimes grades are deferred until a final portfolio of a student's best work from the quarter or the semester is turned in at the end of the course. At that time, they might be graded by you, or they might be graded by a departmental portfolio system where you and your colleagues grade each other's papers.

Such a course design allows students to work on individual projects since the material covered is not presented in a lecture format. There are, however, many possible ways of organizing such a course. You might ask the students to browse through the table of contents of the text and list the chapters they are interested in in order of preference. If you choose this method, you can divide the class into groups according to their interests. Each group reads, talks, and writes about material in which they are interested. Periodically, groups share their information with the entire class through oral presentations on the readings, sharing of drafts, and so forth. This organization allows students not only to follow their own interests, but through the reports of other students also exposes them to more of the book than can be covered in a traditional course. Sometimes this sharing motivates them to want to read other materials. We have taught classes where students read many readings that weren't specifically assigned because other students' responses kindled their interest. Additionally, students usually read and write more effectively when they are personally attracted to the material and when they have a choice in selecting it.

An alternate method that allows for student choice but keeps the class working together would have students rank the chapters according to interest and have the class read the chapters in order of preference. If you choose this method, you can have all students read the entire chapter or form groups of four or five students and divide the chapters. Then students could report to their groups. Since each group will be familiar with the entire chapter, after small-group discussions they can share insights with the entire class.

Another method of organizing the course would be for you to choose the readings, for example, assigning entire chapters, perhaps one from the beginning, middle, and end of the book. Alternately, you can assign selections from each chapter. We do recommend that students read the introductions and the legal documents as well as the final selection in each chapter because they set the historical context that is the framework for the readings included in the chapter. Then they could read all or some of the selections depending on your goals and your students' interests.

At the beginning of the course, you might wish to introduce the general topic of multiethnic courses. Students could generate the arguments for and against a course that focuses on multicultural issues and writers. You could begin by raising some of the following questions to be considered during the semester or quarter:

1. Who should take ethnic literature or history courses? Should they be for members of a particular ethnic group? Should students who enroll in a freshman English class have to read ethnic writers?

2. If classes focus on ethnic issues and are mainly attended by those most interested, members of those groups, do these classes tend to ghettoize minorities on campus?

3. Is a multicultural society a goal we should aim for in America, or are we losing our American identity and values? As we mentioned previously, depending on your student body, students may be resistant to spending a course looking at the immigrant and ethnic experience. Airing these concerns early is one way to explain the purposes of the course and to allow students to vent any resistance.

The Social Context for Writing

Before deciding on the organization of the class, you might want to consider the following factors that we believe can influence learning. We feel that it is important to create a comfortable, safe atmosphere for all students by validating their contributions to the class. In addition, you must constantly be on the alert to try to assess the learning situation for all students, majority as well as minority. One of the reasons that we recommend small-group work and reader responses (to be discussed shortly) is because these activities tend to allow students to comment freely. Students often feel safer talking in a small group out of hearing of the instructor. Since there can be no "wrong" responses, students will become more comfortable about their writing.

You should also consider creating a learning situation that taps the expertise of your students. The material presented in this text focuses on many different cultures. In some cases, your students may be more knowledgeable about those cultures than you are. We hope that your class will provide opportunities for students who are members of particular groups to share that specialized knowledge. However, we also want to make you aware that a single student who is a member of one of these groups may feel uncomfortable asking to be made the representative of an entire group, the "expert" on the situation of African Americans or Japanese Americans, for instance.

One natural response to reading about an unfamiliar culture is the forming of generalizations and opinions about the culture as a whole. But you need to caution students to take care not to stereotype. A discussion of the individual variation that takes place within cultural boundaries will help students understand that while people might share a culture and cultural values, every person is different. When speculating about any group, students in your class who are members of that group can comment on the validity of the speculation.

Material such as this may provoke discussions that become controversial. In such discussions, it is very important to help students learn to listen to each other with respect even if they don't agree. You can model this behavior and can reinforce it when you see good examples. Additionally, if problems arise and tempers get out of hand, post-reading class discussions about the breakdown in communications can clear the air and help students understand the dynamics of the interaction. Sometimes this discussion can take place immediately. Sometimes it is better to let tempers cool and have the discussion at the next class meeting. You have to judge the mood of the class. An alternative might be to have students write a journal entry about the discussion, citing where misunderstandings occurred and so forth. When things go wrong, discussing them openly often works much better than trying to ignore problems and leaving some students feeling resentful. Another method that promotes understanding is asking students to write about topics from multiple perspectives. Having to write from another person's position will often help reveal another point of view.

Teaching Strategies

We want to describe briefly some of the teaching strategies that we recommend as well as some additional activities we believe help enrich the learning experience.

Active Reading We hope that students will actively interact with texts by outlining, taking notes, and using other strategies. One technique that works well to further recall and analyze is "paragraph glossing." This strategy is particularly helpful with a difficult reading and can be done in class or as a homework assignment. Paragraph glossing can be organized in the following ways. One student can gloss an entire essay, or only a page, or a single paragraph. Sometimes two students can work together with beneficial results. An individual student can read the paragraph and write a sentence that summarizes the content of that paragraph. For a classroom activity, one or a group of two students can be assigned a page of a text so that someone is glossing each page. Students can usually gloss a page in about twenty minutes. Then the students can read their glosses in order or put them on the board. This way the entire class can see an outline of the main ideas of a difficult piece of writing. The glosses can also provide a natural lead-in for discussion since students have chosen what they believe is important. Students can also challenge each other's interpretation. For students who have difficulty reading university material, using this technique adds to their ability to comprehend material, to see how an essay is put together, and to write their own essays.

Small-Group Activities Small-group discussion and other collaborative reading and writing activities break the pattern. of teacher-directed activities. When activities are teacher-directed, discussion participation is often limited to a few (usually the same) students. Instead, the class can be broken up into groups for discussion, for activities such as paragraph glossing, or jigsawing (dividing reading material into parts with each student in a group reading a part and them summarizing it for the members of the group), or collaborative writing assignments.

Groups can be formed at random, for example, students can be directed to form a group with the students sitting next to them or with students working on the same essay topic. In classrooms where there are tables and movable chairs, small groups are easy to form. Classrooms with fixed desks (anathema for the composition teacher) require more ingenuity. Students are often quite willing to sit on tables or the floor. Each group can be given the same or a different question orally or on a slip of paper. Usually, the group or the teacher appoints one person to record the discussion and to report on it at the end of the class. The teacher usually circulates to answer questions, listen in, and keep groups on task.

Small-group activities have many benefits. They encourage shy students to participate. Students who participate in groups usually have more of a sense of the classroom as a writing community.

Reading Logs   Reader-response journals are a way for students to write down their responses to a particular reading, therefore allowing them to formulate their ideas about the reading, react to it, and so forth. This journal can then be used as the basis for class discussion about the reading or as a place for working through ideas for more formal papers. These can follow several formats. Students can write a response to each reading assignment of at least a page. A response can vary from a summary of the material, to a personal memory elicited by the reading, to questions that the student has about the reading, to a formal analysis of the material. Usually, the directions include asking students to notice something in the reading and respond to it. You might encourage students to discuss a point made by the reading and comment on it by relating it to a personal experience, analyzing the point, or discussing it in a way that shows some careful thinking about the issues raised. Sometimes responses focus on parts of the reading that move the students or make them angry. Try to help students report these responses and also to analyze why they responded the way they did. If students bring their responses to class, they can read them aloud in small groups and then use them to initiate discussion. If students feel that their responses are too personal to share with the group, they can be collected by the teacher every week or two and read. Responses are never graded or corrected for grammar or spelling. The teacher can make an overall comment, usually addressed to the student by name and signed by the teacher. The comment might respond to questions or acknowledge the student's contribution but also might include suggestions regarding content and development.

An alternate method of using reader responses is to have students write a ten-minute response to the reading in class. Then circulate the responses so that everyone reads all of them. As the teacher reads the responses, she or he can note points to bring up in the following class discussion. Alternately, responses can be circulated in a small group and form the basis for their discussion, which is then reported to the class.

Dialogues   Another way of beginning discussion about a reading is through the use of a dialogue. Several of the questions in the text direct the students to use this technique. A dialogue pairs students, usually at random. You can begin the dialogue, which might take place, for example, between two authors or two characters in a reading, or by writing the first lines on the board. The partner in the dialogue then responds in the character of the author, character, and so on. Partner one answers the response as she or he believes her or his character would. Students usually can continue writing the dialogue for fifteen to twenty minutes. Then each pair can read its creation aloud to the class. Students often want to read their own parts, and they often read them with expression, making for a lively class session. We have been amazed at the variation of the final results.

Dialogues can reveal points of view of the characters or spark debates about the appropriateness of the imagined responses. Would this author or character have responded in this way and why or why not are possible follow-up questions.

You can also use the dialogue to discuss other issues that come up in class. For example, you can assign a dialogue between two authors in response to a point that comes up in discussion.

Students really seem to enjoy the dialogue, and the results indicate a richness of response that is unavailable in large-group discussions.

We hope you will feel free to experiment with these techniques and to vary them as suits you and your students. We also want to encourage you to also allow students to design their own reading and writing activities.

PART II
CHAPTER NOTES

CHAPTER 1

POINTS OF ENTRY, POINTS OF DEPARTURE

This opening chapter differs from the openings in the other two editions of *American Mosaic.* Here we want to introduce students to some of the larger issues that surround past and present immigration to the United States and our resulting diverse society. In order to do that we have chosen readings from a variety of voices, perspectives, and time periods. Emma Lazarus's poem "The New Colossus" speaks of a "nation of immigrants," but Joseph Bruchac's poem "Ellis Island" reminds us of those people whom the immigrants displaced. Greg Sarris and Henry Louis Gates Jr. also speak for those "others" who were forced out of their homes and their homelands to unwillingly become part of this "nation of immigrants." And even for immigrants, life is not always easy in the United States as Eva Hoffman, an immigrant from Poland, explains. Larger issues involving the effect of immigration and diversity on American society in general are debated in the readings by Francis Fukuyama and Arnold Krupat.

This chapter also explores some of the words associated with the concept of "multiculturalism." Terms such as *melting pot, the American Dream, manifest destiny, assimilation, acculturation, political correctness* and *family values* are often used by students though they may have very little knowledge of their origin and meaning. The introduction to the chapter and the reading by James Truslow Adams define and set some of these words in a rich historical context. Such a setting helps students see how the terms were created, thus helping them see them as products of a period rather than integral parts of the American psyche.

You might begin by listing these terms and others from the introduction on the board and have students work individually or in small groups to define them. They can then share their definitions with the class. A discussion of where they think the terms came from can follow the discussion of what the terms mean. Students can then go home and research the terms. When they return to class, they can compare what they found out with what they had thought the terms meant. Often their understanding of these terms is very limited and a class discussion clarifying some of the meanings will greatly enhance their ability to read and understand the texts. One term that has a great deal of resonance for students is the term, *the American Dream.* The Adams reading introduces that term and you might wish to assign it next. In fact, you might design the course, itself, around the theme of the American Dream. Students can consider what the dream is, what it means, and how well that dream has been realized by various ethnic groups.

EMMA LAZARUS
The New Colossus (p. 10)

Students will probably be familiar with at least part of this poem. In fact, they may be so familiar with the poem that they may not have thought much about what it is saying. They might want to share their associations (the journal assignment) with the class. Students can also bring in commercial uses of the symbol for the Statue of Liberty and discuss the appropriateness of using the symbol for those purposes. You might wish to introduce this poem with the Bruchac poem and compare them. Does the poem romanticize and sentimentalize immigrants as the introduction to the chapter suggests? Students might want to discuss this statement and present evidence supporting their point of view.

Hopefully, all of your students will have access to the Internet. If they do not, have some students do research and bring in the materials to the class.

Students who wish to answer question 4 should be directed to Peter Schuck's article "Border Crossing," in chapter 9, which reviews immigration law.

JOSEPH BRUCHAC
Ellis Island (p. 11)

If you are interested in using this poem and the previous one to teach literary concepts, you might want to focus on the imagery in both (question 2). Students can begin by defining the literary terms and then finding examples in the poems. If they have done the journal entry, they might want to analyze their own writing and identify the images there.

Question 4 focuses on the wider meaning of the poem. You may want to have students think about their own attitudes toward the United States and the attitudes they learned in their history classes in elementary and high school. Was this a vast open land just waiting to be occupied? What rights did the people who lived here before the settlers came have? Settlers certainly cultivated and developed the land. Did this give them rights of ownership? Such a discussion may help students prepare for the readings in the American Indian chapter.

JAMES TRUSLOW ADAMS
From The Epic of America (p. 13)

Adams is credited with having introduced the phase "the American Dream" in this book. In the journal entry, students can define the term for themselves and compare their definition with Adams's. Students can then share their entries with the class. In the discussion that follows try to make students aware of Adams's attitudes toward Indians, whom he calls savages. We considered cutting this part of the selection but decided to leave it in because we feel it's important for students to understand the contradictions in someone like Adams. On the one hand, he seems to be advocating freedom and equality for everyone, yet on closer examination his American Dream seems to be only for white men and occasionally women. In addition, Adams was writing at a time when segregation was rampant in the United States, and he makes no mention of that bar to equality. These contradictions will also become evident if students do the group assignment on Adams's values.

Essay question 3 allows students to not only write about Adams's views but also to share their own. Students might want to view the film *American Dream* and use that as an example of how Americans are losing the dream. On the other hand, some of the nightly news programs feature continuing segments that reflect how many people are achieving the American Dream. Students can use examples from these sources or their own experience to support their points.

Question 4 gives students an opportunity to explore and develop an essay about one of the key terms in the reading. Some of my students chose to write about several of the terms and weave them together around the central theme of the American Dream.

HENRY LOUIS GATES Jr.
"What's in a Name?" Some Meanings of Blackness (p. 20)

Gates's essay, like Takaki's in chapter 7, partly deals with the issue of naming. He challenges readers to consider the ways in which specific names reflect the value systems associated with them. If you have not had a discussion about naming and the power conferring names reveals, you should bring up this topic in your pre- or post-reading discussion. Some questions to ask might include: Who does the naming? Do groups have names they use among themselves but that are offensive when used by outsiders? Related issues include negative and positive names, changing names, and names as a reflection of political correctness. Political correctness may be a controversial topic for your class, so you should be prepared for a heated discussion. If you discuss political correctness, question 4 could deal with any aspect of racial conflict, including what students may perceive as reverse racism. Students who have strong feelings about political correctness and reverse racism will probably be more open to the material in this text if they are allowed to discuss these topics openly. Gates himself has been one of the strongest advocates for the position that not only African Americans should teach African American literature. Students might also want to research affirmative action programs on their campus.

Students may need help with vocabulary and concepts in this selection. Question 2 specifically asks them to work together to define these terms. The literary analysis may also be beyond many students' ability and they may need help. They may be stimulated to read the other authors discussed. Questions and class discussion can focus on the larger issues of racism and naming.

GREG SARRIS
Battling Illegitimacy: Some Words Against the Darkness (p. 34)

Students usually find this selection provocative. Sarris, in telling the story of his mixed heritage, raises some central issues and sources of conflict: Who is a legitimate member of an ethnic group, and how is ethnic identity determined? Questions 2 and 4 focus directly on these issues. Your students might want to discuss the appropriateness of revealing so much personal material in an academic essay.

Question 1 invites students to tell their own stories. A topic for further discussion would include the role of storytelling in the family, in the classroom, and in society. Your class might want to combine these or other personal stories into a class text to be photocopied and distributed to all class members.

Question 3 requires students to read the text closely and write an essay based on information from the reading.

EVA HOFFMAN
From Lost in Translation (p. 41)

Hoffman's piece resonates for many students because it deals with the immigrant's conflict of trying to decide between assimilation to a new culture and accommodation. Even students who are not immigrants can identify with her struggles. Many students find the university an alien culture and assimilating into that culture makes them outsiders in their home communities. We found our students, both native-born and immigrants, to be very involved in the issues Hoffman raises and easily able to recognize similar conflicts in their own lives and that of their friends. This leads to lively discussions and papers.

Students enjoyed discussing their journal entries and comparing their attitudes toward various forms of behavior. They might make a list of conflicting responses, such as their response to strangers asking them personal questions, and see if they believe they share the values of their classmates.

Question 3 allows students to discuss Hoffman's conflicts regarding assimilation versus accommodation. This topic is expanded in question 4, where students can talk about the benefits and problems of trying to retain a native culture while also trying to fit into a new one. While question 3 asks students to focus on the text and Hoffman's experience, question 4 encourages them to write about themselves or people they know or have read about.

FRANCIS FUKUYAMA
Immigrants and Family Values (p. 50)

You might want to have students read Fukuyama's essay and Krupat's essay at the same time. Fukuyama challenges "multicultural approaches" to education that he says are detrimental to newcomers. Krupat argues that our modem world with its multicultural environment demands such educational programs.

Our students benefited by glossing each paragraph of this essay. You can have each student do the whole essay or you can make it a classroom exercise where pairs of students are assigned several paragraphs; after glossing, students can share their summaries with the class. The ensuing discussion helps bring up the contradictions in Fukuyama's position.

If you teach the essays together, you can have the students gloss both. These essays could also make an interesting dialogue assignment. Each of a pair of students could represent one of the authors and debate the values of multicultural education. If your students enjoy classroom debates, they could also use the information in the essays as support for each opposing position on the issue of multicultural education. Or students could try to imagine how Krupat would respond to some of Fukuyama's points or vice versa.

The journal entry asks students to explore their feelings about immigration. For further information on immigration laws see Schuck in the last chapter.

Question 3 asks students to read the text carefully, explain it, and respond to it. Question 4 directs students to use their own knowledge to expand on one of the themes introduced in the essay. Some of our students tried to write essays that dealt with several of these themes and that caused some problems. Each topic is very broad and students might be more successful if they focused on one, as the question directs, and really developed it. This would also give them the opportunity to do outside research.

ARNOLD KRUPAT
From **Conclusion: For Multiculturalism** (p. 62)

Reading Krupat helps students grapple with the issues surrounding a multicultural curriculum. This might be a time for them to discuss the reasons why you chose this text and the benefits they can gain by reading works by such diverse authors. They may also have complaints that they want to air. The journal assignment asks them to reflect on the reading they did in high school. For many students, a diet of the "classics" is exactly what they wanted. Others felt excluded because they never read about anyone like themselves. A class discussion focused on these differing viewpoints might clear the air and would certainly help students understand another's perspective.

A writer's and a reader's perspective is a central issue in question 3. If students select this essay, make sure they take into account when the particular poetry was written. Did the historical context shape the author's perspective? How do we view the work today? How has our historical context shaped our perspective?

Question 4 allows students to use their knowledge and imaginations and design curriculum for a university literature class. The letter format helps establish awareness of audience.

Connecting (p. 71)

Critical Thinking and Writing

In this section we have tried to raise student awareness of some current issues such as immigrants and immigration policy, assimilation vs. accommodation, the ways we think and talk about indigenous peoples. The connecting questions ask students to reflect on these issues, on the situation of recent immigrants, and changing attitudes toward immigrants and diversity (questions 1–4). Question 5 suggests that students will learn a great deal by actually interviewing an immigrant and writing about her experience. Question 6 is also not a traditional essay question. It allows writers to create a dialogue between speakers with opposing viewpoints. Question 10 asks students to use personal evidence to support a point, modeling their essay on Gates, Sarris, and Hoffman.

CHAPTER 2

AMERICAN INDIANS: RECLAIMING CULTURAL HERITAGE

This chapter deals with writing by American Indian writers from the late 1870s to the period that has been called the Native American Renaissance, an outgrowth of the civil rights movement of the 1960s. The rebirth of interest in American Indian culture and in American Indian voices reflects a general awareness in Americans of the importance of cultural heritage and the movement toward cultural pluralism and away from a melting-pot mentality.

Before we begin our discussion of the selections in this chapter, we want to explain our choice of the term American Indian over Native American. We have chosen to use *American Indian* because it is more current. Some writers alternate names, but we felt that would be confusing for students. In addition, Native American can refer to anyone born in the United States, so the name might be confusing to students. Current legal decisions have also mandated the term *American Indian* in some court cases involving land or usage rights.

The introduction reviews the history of tribal contact with the white man and the resulting difficulties of the tribes in maintaining land, heritage, and even family. Each of the authors represented in the chapter is from a different tribe. It is important for students to realize that American Indians are not all the same but come from diverse tribes and cultures. Students should read the introduction but might discuss the Beginning exercise beforehand.

Because students have probably been exposed to images of American Indians in the media, they may feel they know a great deal about them. For example, American Indians have recently begun to be portrayed as protectors of the natural environment. Is this a realistic or romanticized portrayal? This Beginning exercise is designed to alert students to the diversity that exists among American Indians, just as it does among other groups, and to help them avoid stereotypes that "portray" living American Indians as either drunken savages or enlightened ecologists. Encourage students to explore their preconceptions and to check them with the portrayals in the readings.

From The Indian Removal Act (p. 84)

The document presented here is a section of the Indian Removal Act of 1830. We felt that it is an important reading because it clearly exemplifies how the American government treated American Indians. It also focuses on the potential effect of forced removal on a people's sense of identity. Students might begin the discussion by talking about what it means to leave one's ancestral lands. Some students may have ancestors who endured forced emigration (e.g., Africans forced to leave

Africa or others forced to emigrate by political or religious persecution). The Deloria and Lytle selection at the end of this chapter chronicles many of the broken promises between the United States government and the tribes. If your students would like to concentrate on the government's treatment of American Indians, they may wish to discuss possible motivations the government had for uprooting entire nations in this way before reading.

Implicit in the act was the belief that American Indians would soon become extinct. The Responding questions aim to make students aware of this by having them look closely at the language and construction of the document. Section 3 provides that lands shall revert to the United States "if the Indians become extinct, or abandon the same." If your class talked about the effects of being forced from ancestral lands, you may want to discuss how such a separation could contribute to the extinction of a people.

CHIEF JOSEPH
From An Indian's View of Indian Affairs (p. 86)

This reading gives students a chance to revisit the westward migration of settlers from the Indian's point of view. Many students, by now, are more understanding of the injustices indigenous peoples faced on this continent, but few may have had an opportunity to hear an Indian comment on the fate of his people.

This might be a good opportunity to begin talking about perspective. The journal entry asks students to consider whose perspective shaped the history they learned in school. As they work on the group assignment, they can begin to construct that history from the Indians' point of view. Students might want to think about other examples where perspective influences what is taught.

Question 3 gives students an opportunity to study Chief Joseph's speech from a rhetorical perspective. Students may want to list possible rhetorical strategies as a pre-writing assignment.

Question 4 asks readers to compare Chief Joseph's values with those expressed the Bill of Rights and then to judge who lived more in accord with those values. Students may be surprised at how closely the values of Chief Joseph and the Bill of Rights resemble each other. They may also be discouraged by the actions of the government in relation to the Indians. They might want to consider other instances when the government did not give its citizens the protection they deserved. You could open that topic as a question and see what students know about the treatment of minorities in this country. This could lead students into any of the other chapters because each contains examples of injustices and prejudice. However, students particularly interested in government policy could be directed to the chapters on the Chinese, Japanese, and African Americans.

D'ARCY McNICKLE
Train Time (p. 90)

This story continues the discussion about perspective as it deals with the differing viewpoints of two cultures. Questions 2 and 3 directly ask students to explore these varying perspectives. Question 4 allows them to confront the issues involved in being forced to adapt to another culture. Your students may not be aware of the government policy of removing Indian children from their families and sending them to boarding school. This story allows them to see why people from the mainstream culture may have felt that they were giving children opportunities that otherwise would have been denied them, but it also allows them to see some of the poignancy and heartbreak for the children who were sent away.

LESLIE MARMON SILKO
Lullaby (p. 95)

This touching story illustrates some of the difficulties American Indians experienced as a result of the government policies presented in the introduction. It also deals with a number of the themes that have been explored throughout the text: the problems that can develop when people of a minority culture don't speak the same language or live by the same customs as those in the majority culture, the frustrations in dealing with a bureaucracy, the loss of children to a "foreign" culture, the inability of minority members to become fully accepted by the mainstream even if they do follow the "rules."

A pre-reading activity might be a discussion and sharing of experiences in which a misunderstanding of language and customs created difficulties. After students have read the essay, questions 1 and 2 can give them a creative means to explore this problem through writing. It could also lead to a discussion of the rights of the state versus the rights of the family. Students might be able to bring in current news stories about American Indian tribes who have struggled to reclaim children who have been adopted away from the tribe. Question 1 could serve as a ten-minute, in-class writing assignment. Students can also write about their emotional responses to the story.

One approach to this reading would involve looking at the problems created by the inability to communicate, both linguistically and conceptually. Another possibility is to discuss the problems people sometimes have when dealing with a bureaucracy like the government or the university. A follow-up discussion could touch on the government's point of view and the arguments on Ayah's side. A possible discussion or debate topic would be the right of institutions to interfere in family life for the good of minor children. The parents' plight could be compared to the plight of the family in Sui Sin Far's "In the Land of the Free" in chapter 2. The children in both stories have, in effect, been stolen from their parents and their culture.

Another approach is to look at this story from the point of view of those who try to assimilate and become part of the mainstream. Chato worked well in the white man's world, but in the end he still is thrown aside. Question 3 is helpful in exploring this issue.

JAMES WELCH
Plea to Those Who Matter (p. 103)

Students should be made aware of the social pressures on American Indians to conform to Euro American standards of beauty and behavior. This is an issue that has faced and still faces members of ethnic minorities. In Thurman's *The Blacker the Berry* in chapter 5, the heroine values lighter skin and what she feels is appropriate behavior. All ethnic groups have been pressured at one time or another to straighten hair and noses, lighten skin, and tone down behavior to fit an Anglo-Saxon image. Movements such as the "Black is Beautiful movement" of the 1960s tried to counter that pressure. A pre-reading discussion could focus on these issues or ask students if they have ever felt that they had to strive for a certain image. We've had students tell us that criteria such as the above still influence self-image. Question 1 could be used as a follow-up activity.

LOUISE ERDRICH
From Love Medicine (p. 104)

This novel has recently been reissued in an expanded form. However, this chapter remains the same. Because of the novel's structure, this chapter can stand alone and be enjoyed as a short story.

One pre-reading activity asks students to think about a time when they tried to do something to help someone and everything went wrong. You might ask them how they felt when their good intentions went awry. This is what happens to Lipsha Morrissey, but from the experience he reaches a new understanding of life, death, and love. A post-reading discussion might begin by talking about, or writing about in a ten-minute, in-class writing, what he learned. Question 4 extends the discussion of what Lipsha has learned, and the students could use the in-class discussion as pre-writing for a formal paper.

Another aspect of this story you may wish to concentrate on is Lipsha's belief in "the touch" and how he reconciles it with Christianity. Questions 2 and 3 can be helpful in exploring this theme.

Students who enjoy this selection might want to read the entire novel or Erdrich's other novels about the same group of characters.

PAULA GUNN ALLEN
Pocahontas to Her English Husband, John Rolfe (p. 122)

Your students will probably be familiar with the Disney version of Pocahontas. Some may have been inspired to consult the history books to check its accuracy. The journal entry lets students write out their version of her story. Students can share what they know and compare it to a version from an encyclopedia. Then they can compare these versions with the Pocahontas of the poem. A further discussion of the differences between versions leads to question 4 that asks students to evaluate the importance of presenting historical myths accurately. The class could break into groups and research some of our society's myths as a pre-writing exercise.

Question 3 refers students to the text and asks them to support their conclusions about Pocahontas's attitude toward her husband with textual evidence.

SIMON J. ORTIZ
The Language We Know (p. 124)

This selection, like many of the others in this chapter, deals with language. Ortiz directly explores the role language plays in defining heritage. Students might want to compare his views of the uses of language with Sarris's storytelling.

Question 1 serves as a pre-reading activity because it invites students to think about the role writing serves in their lives. This could be broadened to include a discussion of different types of writing (formal versus informal, for example) and differing audiences. Your students might want to focus more directly on their own writing processes and the way those change in relation to the task and the audience.

If your class wants to explore the differences between orality and literacy, they should work on question 2. This will also help prepare them to write the formal essay required to answer question 3. Though most of the information needed to answer this question is available through close reading of the text, the last part of the question asks students to consider the differences between a written and an oral version of a story. Students may also want to discuss what might be lost when a story is written down.

If you wish to take this topic further, you can initiate a discussion of written versus oral history. Students might want to discuss the effect of published versions of a historical event, the influence of the author on the reporting of an event, and the possibility of multiple versions of events. These topics may take your students too far afield here but might be interesting to discuss as an overview to the text (see the introduction to this manual).

Question 4 raises a broader issue: the necessity for a mainstream education in order to achieve power in this society. This subject could be used as the topic of an in-class debate. Students may have their own personal conflicts revolving around this subject and may welcome an opportunity to air them. Related issues include standard English versus dialect, dress and behavioral codes, joining the mainstream or fighting against it from the outside.

VINE DELORIA JR. AND CLIFFORD M. LYTLE
A Status Higher Than States (p. 132)

We included this selection because it traces the history of the negotiations that have taken place between the federal government and the tribes. Students might want to look at this selection and explore how the point of view of the authors (one is an American Indian) influences the presentation of the material. Questions to consider include: Is the American Indian point of view present in traditional histories written by authors from the dominant culture? What is included in this text that might be left out of histories written by authors from the dominant culture?

Even if you are not interested in discussing the topics mentioned above, the selection works well as a historical overview and probably contains information unfamiliar to most students. Questions 1 and 2 ask students to engage with the material and, after rewriting the provisions in simpler language, create a time line so they can see the long history of these negotiations. Your students may want to add other important historical events to the time line so they can understand the context of relations between the American government and the American Indian tribes. What was going on in the nation and the world during the same period as the treaty negotiations?

Questions 3 and 4 raise the issues of self-rule. Students need to understand that all American Indians and all tribes do not think alike. Arguing as a traditional or a militant American Indian will help them see events from a multiplicity of viewpoints. A recurring reminder is necessary to keep students aware that a culture may have certain characteristics and that people within a culture may share certain values, but individuals within a group vary greatly. In addition, what we may think of as a manifestation of the culture may only be the idiosyncrasy of a few individuals.

LINDA HOGAN
Crossings (p. 145)

This poem explores some of the ways in which elements of the physical world can prompt a connection between personal and collective histories. The questions encourage students to explore their relationship to nature. At the same time, they encourage students to use their imaginations. This would be a good assignment for students who would like to try their hand at some creative writing.

The group assignments let students verbalize their beliefs about Indians and check them against some factual evidence.

NICOLE BRODEUR
The Meaning of the Hunt (p. 147)

This piece and the one that follows both relate to current events in the life of the Makahs and their desire to resume whaling. They center on conflicts between traditional practices and current conservation efforts by the American government. You might want to have your students read them together. The questions ask students to think about the role of tradition in their own lives and in the lives of the Makahs, so that they can understand that each culture has traditions that might seem strange or even harmful to others. They might even brainstorm a list of practices that are culturally specific such as plural marriages, circumcision, clitorectemy, and so forth. When should government interfere and when should it protect a group's right to practice their own traditions?

Question 4 asks students to consider the difficulties of maintaining traditional practices when they are not the practices of the dominant culture. Students can apply this example to many other groups or even to their own personal beliefs and traditions.

You might want your students to debate some of the issues that these readings address.

JERRY LARGE
Concerning a Whale (p. 150)

If you have already discussed the larger issues involved with whaling, you might want to spend most of your discussion on Large's comments quoted in questions 3 and 4. Students can voice their own feelings about endangered species and then decide whether Large's charges of indifference to nonwhites are fair. Students might want to consider whether Large's position as a person of color makes his argument stronger.

Connecting (p. 153)

Critical Thinking and Writing

All of the sets of Connecting questions are designed to point up relationships within chapters as well as across the text. Students should be encouraged to use these questions as topics for formal papers or as models for designing their own questions. They force students to think about broader issues and to acknowledge the similarities of experiences among many diverse groups. The Connecting questions ask students to reconsider the role of tradition in indigenous cultures and the difficulties of maintaining those traditions. Questions 2, 4, 8, and 9 deal directly with issues of tradition, accommodation, and assimilation. Other questions ask students to consider the role and contribution of Indians to life in America.

Questions 5 and 6 focus on the contributions of American Indians and ask students to reconsider their portrayal in the media. Students need to be made aware that the portrayal of American Indians changed after the 1960s. Prior to the greater awareness of civil rights issues, American Indians were usually portrayed as savages harming innocent white settlers. Students might want to outline that history. Now that students have read all the selections, they can compare their preconceptions with these portraits and think about all of our tendencies to generalize about groups from the actions of some individuals or some segments of the group.

The Research questions in this section ask students to either look back into the history of an American Indian leader or to look forward to the situation of American Indians today. Some students may be interested in these topics. All questions could be scaled down to be manageable as a paper topic assignment. Students should be encouraged to use these questions as a springboard or a model for their own questions.

CHAPTER 3

EARLY IMMIGRANTS: IN SEARCH OF THE LAND OF MILK AND HONEY

This chapter chronicles the struggles of several representative groups of early immigrants to the East Coast of the United States. Their triumphs and trials are repeated in the experience of other groups throughout the text. This period 1820–1920 was marked by a wave of immigration to the United States not only of Europeans but also of the first Arab immigrants. In addition, this period saw the beginning of the debate between the ideals of nativism and cultural pluralism. Students, however, should be reminded that there were many willing and unwilling immigrants to this country before the 1820s who with the original inhabitants and later immigrants make up the American mosaic.

The introduction to this chapter tries to set the scene for the reader by explaining the political and economic conditions in Europe and the Middle East that prompted the large wave of immigration. Reading the introduction will help students understand the mind-set of the writers of the period, so they should read it before reading any of the selections. Many of your students will have some kind of personal connection with immigrants of this period—whether they are the great-grandchildren of the immigrants or descendants of people already here who found themselves with new competition for jobs, housing, and power. Since it presents the reasons for this wave of immigration and the conditions that met the new arrivals, the introduction may engage students' interest or help them recall their own family stories about the immigration experience.

One of the themes that emerges and recurs throughout the book is the question of assimilation. You may wish to explore this topic. When looking at assimilation, it may be interesting to discuss why some immigrants are highly motivated to enter the American mainstream while others are just as determined to retain traditional ways. Their situation can also be contrasted with other groups who were unwilling immigrants to the United States, such as Africans (brought as slaves), American Indians (immigrants through conquest), and Mexicans (who suddenly found themselves living in the United States). Students who are the children of recent immigrants or who are immigrants themselves might want to compare the experiences of their families. If time permits, students could be encouraged to interview family members and gather family stories or mementos to share with the class and to aid in the Beginning exercise. A discussion of the introduction should lead naturally into the Beginning exercise.

We recommend setting aside one class period for this discussion as it can set up the context for reading the whole chapter. We like dividing the class into small groups and letting each group speculate about reasons for emigrating. One source of information for the discussion would be the introduction, but another rich source would be the student's own knowledge. Some students might remember facts from a history class. Others might have talked to parents and grandparents about the reasons why their families came to America.

Next students could discuss what they think was particularly appealing about America as a destination. Again the introduction is a resource. But let them speculate about the political, economic, and social conditions that existed in this country in 1820. If students generate questions, such as who was president, what were immigration policies, and so forth, they can find the answers in their school library before the next class meeting. Different classes will take the discussion in different directions, and that should be encouraged. American Indian or African American students might bring up their history in America, which of course predates this period. If students don't bring up this issue, you might want to point out the contrast between immigrants who chose to come to America, the Promised Land, and those who were forced to come to live in hardship as slaves or those who were already here and were persecuted by the newcomers.

After twenty minutes, one member of each group can summarize its discussion for the class while you or a student records the main points on the board. These can then be used as the basis for a general discussion. This exercise can segue into a discussion of the Bill of Rights, which certainly might be discussed as one of the factors that made coming to America so desirable.

The Bill of Rights (p. 165)

The Bill of Rights, added to the Constitution in 1791, is a clear statement of the rights guaranteed to citizens. Because of this, many immigrants who were fleeing repressive regimes or religious persecution saw in it the promise of America. We felt it was an appropriate selection because it so clearly represents the ideal of freedom associated with the United States. In addition, the Bill of Rights is an important touchstone for the entire text, which reports numerous violations of the rights guaranteed as well as numerous incidents where the Bill of Rights was used to protect minority groups. If students are familiar with the Bill of Rights, they will have a better understanding of the struggles of various groups to preserve these rights. As a pre-reading assignment you might ask students to write out as many of the provisions of the Bill of Rights as they know. Then they can compare their lists with the document. As a post-reading discussion, you might consider asking students to contrast the Bill of Rights with the protection afforded citizens in any of the European countries during the 1800s. In countries that protected the rights of citizens (Britain, for example) the motivation for emigrating would probably be economic.

If your students have trouble internalizing the meaning of the articles, you may want to ask them to write for ten minutes on question 1. If students are ready for a more complex assignment, question 3 can be used as a post-reading activity. It asks students to move away from the literal meaning of the document and speculate on its significance in a more specific context. The in-class writing or discussion can serve as pre-writing for the formal essay. Students could be asked why the Bill of Rights might have been an incentive for immigration. Then student responses could be read aloud and used as the basis for further discussion.

CONSTANTINE PANUNZIO
In the American Storm (p. 167)

In this selection from his book *The Soul of an Immigrant* Panunzio recounts his somewhat harrowing adventures when he first arrives in America from Italy. As a pre-reading activity, the instructor might want to set the scene by asking students to imagine that they have just arrived in a strange country with little money, little knowledge of the language, and no job or place to stay.

Ask them to think about how they would feel. Brainstormed responses might be jotted down on the board and saved. After the students have read the selection, they can begin discussion by comparing their responses to Panunzio's.

If you use this pre-reading activity, questions 1 and 2 can be helpful as post-reading activities. Question 1 focuses on the story as a stimulus for personal writing, requires an understanding of and a summary of Panunzio's experiences, and some analysis of either a family or an individual experience. Since it is personal, students have a lot of leeway and could, for example, compare Panunzio's experience with their own experience first leaving home and coming to college. This might work well either as a journal entry or as a formal paper. Question 2 asks the students to continue focusing on the experiences of the narrator while encouraging them to think about their own responses and to give reasons why she made her choice.

Questions 3 and 4 require more outside knowledge but can be helpful in developing a more thorough understanding of the period. As such, they might work well in a class discussion where the resources of many students and the teacher can be tapped. Otherwise, they can provide a topic for students who want to do additional research.

Other readings with similar themes of arrival and settling in a new country include Young Yu in chapter 4 and Hijuelos in chapter 9.

OLE EDVART RÖLVAAG
Facing the Great Desolation (p. 175)

This excerpt is interesting because it presents a reluctant pioneer, Beret, who unlike so many heroines of film and story, wishes she were elsewhere and has a great deal of difficulty adjusting to life on the prairie. Her husband, on the other hand, thrives on the adventure, traveling around while she is left to cope with the house and children. It's not surprising that she loses control.

Beret's struggle with self-control and loneliness and with external elements as she attempts to create a community in the wilderness are possible themes for exploration and discussion. The special difficulties for both male and female immigrants are highlighted in this excerpt. If you wish to concentrate on the issue of gender, a pre-reading activity might ask students to discuss the different challenges faced by men and women. The post-reading discussion might focus around question 2, which deals with gender roles within the culture during this period. It is important for students to see this family in its cultural context and to understand that their gender roles were culture specific.

If you wish to explore the unique difficulties that new immigrants may have had in becoming pioneers, you might want to use a pre-reading assignment that asks students to brainstorm about the pressures that all pioneers experienced. For a post-reading exercise, you may want to look at questions 1 and 3 to help in examining the pressures on Beret and Per Hansa and the different ways they dealt with those pressures. This could also lead into question 4, which asks students to compare Beret with the stereotypical pioneer heroine.

Other readings with a similar theme of women challenged by circumstances are Yezierska in chapter 3 and Mohr in chapter 6.

ANZIA YEZIERSKA
The Fat of the Land (p. 187)

We found this story very touching. Students, however, might have a harder time identifying with the mother than we did. Readers need to be sympathetic to Hanneh Breineh to appreciate her predicament at the end of the story, but they also need to understand how she treated the children when they were young and the effects that had on their relationships. Again some pre-reading activity might help. Some discussion of conditions for new immigrants in New York and reference to the pictures in the text would help. The Flynn piece is a good resource. Class discussion about the difficulties of raising a large family on a meager income might set the scene. Perhaps some class discussion about what such a family might wish for in the future would prepare them for the ironic turn of events.

Your students might need help with the pronunciation of characters' names as well as the Yiddish words. A dictionary will provide pronunciations, or perhaps someone in the class will have that expertise. Yezierska translates the Yiddish curses verbatim. Students need to know that they suffer in translation but make sense in the original language.

A post-reading discussion can center around Hanneh's relationship with her children both before and after "making it. " Students could work in groups to discuss to what extent the distance between the mother and children was caused by Hanneh's treatment of them when they were young or her insistence on holding on to her old ways when they are older. Questions 1 and 3 explore these different angles.

Question 1 asks students to take the point of view of one of the other characters in the story. The letter format is often an effective one because it allows the writer to become part of a rhetorical situation and enables her to visualize her audience.

If you have discussed during pre-reading, the issue of poverty and what a family like the Breinehs might aspire to, question 4 could be used as a short in-class writing assignment to begin a post-reading discussion. Since the idea of "making it" occurs throughout the text, the drafts could later be expanded into longer essays possibly comparing the Breinehs' experience with other immigrant families such as those in Hijuelos's "Visitors, 1965" in chapter 9.

Another post-reading discussion might begin by relating Hanneh's situation to Beret's in "'Facing the Great Desolation," pointing up the difficulties for woman immigrants in general and mothers of small children in particular. Students might also want to consider the psychological effect on her of not being needed anymore after having been forced to be so resourceful in her younger days.

Cofer in chapter 4 presents another example of a similar mother/daughter conflict that pits holding on to tradition against becoming part of the mainstream.

ELIZABETH GURLEY FLYNN
From I Speak My Own Piece (p. 204)

This excerpt presents the story of Flynn's family and the political and economic factors that necessitated their emigration from Ireland at the turn of the century. Questions 1 and 2 encourage students to compare the experiences of the Irish with those of recent immigrants to the United States. For many students, the discrimination against the Irish will be new information, and a discussion about the problems they faced may open up a discussion of the hardships most new immigrants had to deal with and the strategies they used for overcoming them. In addition, the reading raises the issue of discrimination along class lines within a group. The situation among the Irish can be compared. to other instances of intergroup prejudice (see for example Thurman, chapter 5, and Islas, chapter 8).

The Flynn excerpt also gives students a sense of conditions in the city during this period and the forces that created these conditions. A post-reading discussion might focus on some of the factors that caused these conditions and compare them to conditions in urban areas today, trying to draw parallels between that period and current conditions in the projects or with the homeless. Bearing these in mind, one question students might want to consider is whether or not things are truly better for immigrants and the poor now than they were in Flynn's time.

Students who live in rural areas or students in cities who have been sheltered may be unaware of the poor living conditions that exist in many urban areas. Students in the class who are more aware may be used as resources. Those who come from poorer families may feel comfortable sharing stories about their communities, but they should never be pressured to do so. Other resources are the media.

Question 4 asks students to think about the issue of responsibility. Today there is more of a public discussion of the responsibilities of landlords. Some slumlords have been in the news because they have been sentenced to live in their own slums. Students can compare ideas about responsibility in our time with those at the turn of the century

Question 3 raises what may be a more controversial issue—the stereotype of the Irish as heavy drinkers. Grandfather Flynn "built a new cabin . . . by setting up a keg of whiskey and inviting all hands to help him" (paragraph 7). Whether or not students bring up this issue, you might want to raise it for discussion. You can begin by talking about stereotypes, how they develop, and the harm they do. Then you could move the discussion on to particulars: reasons people might have been willing to help him for a drink of whiskey, the social and emotional causes of alcohol abuse, the role of alcohol in our society.

MAXINE S. SELLER
Beyond the Stereotype: A New Look at the Immigrant Woman, 1880–1924 (p. 212)

We included this selection because it counteracts the stereotype of immigrant women as backward, ignorant, and degraded. In contrast, it presents the contribution of three dynamic, powerful women from three different ethnic backgrounds. A pre-reading discussion or in-class writing assignment might ask students to describe a typical immigrant woman of this period. What would she be like, and what kind of life would she live? Then, after reading the descriptions aloud in class, students can compare their ideas or create a group profile. This can then be compared to the stereotype Seller presents and the counterexamples she provides. We hope this reading will provoke a discussion that will challenge their preconceptions about immigrants in general and women immigrants in particular, both in the past and today.

Question 1 asks students to describe an immigrant woman and compare her to the stereotype. Here students can use their personal experience, if they wish. If students prefer to distance themselves or have no personal knowledge of immigrants, the option is open for them to write about someone they have read about. Questions 2 through 4 ask students to consider cultural expectations and the influence of cultural and personal factors on development. Such a discussion can move away from the topic of this reading to a discussion of the factors that influence each student's personal development or to the broader issues of nature versus nurture.

JACOB RIIS
Genesis of the Tenement (p. 225)

We have included this excerpt from Riis's book to give students a sense of conditions in New York City during this period and the forces that created those conditions. Further sense of the period can be obtained from the pictures in the text. A pre-reading discussion might begin by looking at the picture of the crowded streets of New York and having students write a short in-class description of what they see. The post-reading activity might elicit parallels between the tenements of that period and conditions faced by residents of today's housing projects or by the homeless. As students read further in the chapter, you might ask them to consider which immigrants they would expect to find inhabiting Riis's tenements.

Questions 1 and 3 try to raise students' awareness of the conditions during Riis's time and those in urban areas today. Considering current conditions in housing projects or with the homeless, one issue students might want to consider is whether or not life is truly better for today's immigrants and the poor now.

Students who live in rural areas or urban students from relatively affluent neighborhoods may be unaware of the squalid living conditions that exist in many poor urban areas. Students who come from poorer families may be invited to share stories about their communities (but they should not be pressured to do so). Students can also look for related stories in the media.

Questions 2 and 4 ask students to think about the issue of landlord responsibility. Students can compare ideas about landlord responsibility in our time with those at the turn of the century.

JAMES WEST DAVIDSON AND MARK HAMILTON LYTLE
Images from the Other Half (p. 230)

This selection is a companion piece to the preceding piece by Jacob Riis as it explores the issues of objectivity and subjectivity in the representation and construction of the immigrant. You might begin with an in-class writing assignment where students write down the impressions of immigrants they gained from reading Riis. Then they can compare their impressions and discuss how closely they believe their views resemble reality. This leads directly into the journal assignment, which asks students to think about the perspective and possible agenda of a photographer. You may want to bring some provocative pictures to class. The essay questions further develop the ideas of illusion versus reality and ask students to consider the perspective of writers and photographers and to think about how public opinion can be shaped by texts and photographs.

ROBERT PINSKY
Shirt (p. 241)

Here is an opportunity for students to become acquainted with Robert Pinsky, who was named poet laureate of the United States for a third year in 1999. They might want to explore how a poet can use a common object as the inspiration for a poem that reflects on the issue of work and the worker. The poem also has a sociohistorical context that helps to illuminate the experience of early as well as current garment workers.

The journal entry asks students to think about employment opportunities for uneducated immigrants to the United States. A class discussion might compare these jobs and working conditions with those of early European immigrants. Then the group assignment asks students specifically to research the Triangle Factory Fire of 1911 and compare it to current headlines about abuses of workers. Essay question 3 gives students the opportunity to use the information from the discussion as the basis of a formal essay.

Question 4 brings up a current moral dilemma by asking students to consider their role as consumers and what responsibility they have for working conditions around the world. If students want to answer this question, they may need to do outside research on working conditions and on the financial realities of the garment industry.

Connecting (p. 244)

Critical Thinking and Writing

The Connecting questions can be used in several ways. You might want to use them to integrate and sum up the chapter. They can serve as discussion topics or as topics for formal essays. We recommend that you let your students choose the questions they wish to write about or let them use these questions as models for ones they will design themselves. The Connecting questions usually cover a broader scope than the Responding questions, which typically ask students to consider one reading. These either ask students to relate large issues within the chapter or across the text. Students might talk or write about these issues as they finish each chapter. If you are using a thematic approach, these questions will help students trace themes throughout the text. If you want students to consider connections within the chapter, refer them to questions 1, 2, 6, and 7. If students are ready to compare readings across the text have them consider questions 9, 10, and 11. For questions that focus on broad general issues, see questions 3, 4, and 5. If you have students who want to deal with topics that require library research, more extensive questions dealing with specific legal and social issues are provided in the section entitled For Further Research.

CHAPTER 4

EARLY CHINESE IMMIGRANTS: THE LURE OF THE GOLD MOUNTAIN

This chapter deals with the immigration of the Chinese to America, which began in the 1840s. Students should read the introduction first because it will help them understand the complex situation of the Chinese in America. On the one hand they were encouraged to come and were praised for their hard work, but at the same time many forces were at work trying to keep them out. This ultimately led to the passage of the Exclusion Act and also prevented the Chinese already in the country from attaining citizenship. The Beginning exercise asks students to flesh out the portrait of the early Chinese immigrants. The goal of the assignment is to make students aware of the hardships these early immigrants had to endure and to think about what would motivate them to attempt such a difficult journey. Since students will discover that these early Chinese were ambitious and hardworking, they should be surprised and question the reasons why they were excluded in 1882. This can lead to a discussion of the Exclusion Act with a focus on why some minority groups are perceived as a threat by the majority.

From The Chinese Exclusion Act (p. 256)

This excerpt depicts the country's fears of the Chinese. As a pre-reading activity, you may want to discuss how the Chinese resistance to assimilation and the "'collective resolve" of the Chinese community may have contributed to the fears. You also may want to discuss how a nation might justify legalizing discrimination.

Question 1 can be used as the topic of a short in-class writing assignment. Alternately, students might want to imagine that they are immigrants from another country (perhaps another Asian country) who hear about the exclusion of the Chinese and discuss what effect, if any, the act has on their decision to immigrate to America. Students may also want to discuss in what ways the act conflicts with the image of America presented by the Bill of Rights in chapter 1.

Three groups can quickly answer the parts A, B, and C of question 2. The groups can then pool their information and use it as background for the essay topic in question 3.

From **The Gold Mountain Poems** (p. 259)

The image of these anonymous writers expressing their disillusion with America by writing poems on a wall is a poignant one. One way to approach this is to look at writing as a way of dealing with frustration. Another approach might be to examine the causes of frustration and disillusionment. Pre-reading might involve a discussion of what students do when they are upset, angry, or frustrated. This could lead to talk about writing as a way of dealing with those feelings. Reading the poems aloud is an effective way of conveying the emotions they express. A different voice should read each poem to emphasize the fact that they are separate poems and could be by three different authors. You may want to discuss the language of the poems. Does it convey a sense of frustration and hopelessness? Question 1 presents a possible follow-up to this approach. It asks the students to take advantage of this form of expression. A side discussion about graffiti (Is it destruction or expression?) might follow.

If you choose to look at the cause of the frustration, you might want to have a pre-reading discussion about the conflicting messages coming from the United States. Chinese were first encouraged to come to the country when cheap labor was needed. Then they were excluded when they were perceived to be a threat. Is there an irony for a country to have both the Bill of Rights and an Exclusion Act? Question 2 is a good starting place for a discussion after reading any of these poems. Question 3 provides a writing assignment that could follow the discussion.

Question 4 asks students to be analytical and persuasive. In order to help them gather evidence for their papers, you might ask if the speakers are justified in their feelings. Was the United States government responsible for the expectations of the immigrants? Or you may want to have pairs of students write a dialogue as preparation with one student acting as the immigrant and the other as the official.

The poems present a specific example of the helplessness and frustrations inflicted on later Chinese immigrants described in the introduction to the chapter. The next story deals with the same theme and might be taught with the poems.

SUI SIN FAR
In the Land of the Free (p. 262)

This is one of the earliest stories by an Asian American writer. Her credentials as an expert in Asian life are somewhat suspect, however, because though she was the child of a Chinese mother, her father was English, and she was raised in America. Her sister, also an author, adopted a Japanese pseudonym. But her work is important because she is one of the first Americans to write from an Asian perspective. Her life is shrouded in mystery. Even her obituary contained misleading information. The family seemed to be trying to hide her Asian heritage. Only recently, through research by S. E. Solberg, are we being presented with a clearer image.

This story illustrates the injustices in the immigration system faced by later Chinese immigrants. A pre-reading discussion might focus on the rights of parents to bring immigrant children to the United States. A broader question might ask if families should have the right to immigrate together. If families must be separated, then what effect does the separation have on family members?

Another pre-reading discussion could focus on how intimidating it is to encounter red tape in a new country with a different language and rules that don't seem to make sense. After reading, question 2 can help students to consider the difficulties faced by people who have to deal with government officials and their vulnerability to exploitation by unscrupulous people. Students might want to compare the problems of later Chinese grants to the reception the pioneer Chinese received or to current immigration stories. Such a discussion might serve as pre-writing for question 1.

If your students are more interested in the theme of loss of culture and identity, they may want to discuss or write about question 4. This theme recurs throughout the text, especially within the context of parent-child relationships. Some students may have experienced or be experiencing these same fears and may be willing to discuss their feelings with the class. Others may feel more comfortable discussing this issue in relation to the story rather than relating it to personal experience.

SHAWN WONG
From Homebase (p. 270)

Students might need some help reading this selection because it makes use of the technique of magic realism to present the speaker's present experience as a journey into the collective past of his ancestors. You might need to explain some elements of magic realism before they begin reading. They might think about what such a technique can add to a story and why a writer would choose to use it. Is the confusion that can result worth the effect it produces? This is a good selection to teach students to be careful readers because if they are not, they probably will not understand what is happening. The group activity gives students an opportunity to review important events in the history of the Chinese in the United States and that should help them understand the story.

Question 3 helps students work through the events in the story by examining the physical and psychological characteristics of the narrator. Question 4 allows students to be creative and to write a similar piece illustrating something about their own history.

MAXINE HONG KINGSTON
The Grandfather of the Sierra Nevada Mountains (p. 279)

This essay, which combines factual and fictionalized episodes, gives a modem perspective on the experience of the Chinese who built the railroads, thus serving to explode the stereotype. Rather than the romanticized vision of happy workers, Kingston outlines the grim reality and danger that faced men like her grandfather. She also explores the way these men suffered from loneliness and loss of identity. Kingston's father had been a "sojourner" from China; her mother had immigrated through Ellis Island. Your students will probably be unaware of the massacres of Chinese workers (that went unpunished). You may want to bring this up before they read the selection.

Question 1 focuses student attention on an important aspect of this reading: the contribution of the Chinese to America. Whether or not students choose to write on this topic, it could be used as a follow-up, small- or large-group discussion topic. Students should be reminded that grandfather couldn't become an American citizen because Asians were unable to obtain citizenship. How was it possible that the country that had the Bill of Rights and the Constitution could deny citizenship to a particular group? Students need to remember that in spite of the Constitution and the Bill of Rights, slavery had also been legal until the 1860s.

Question 2 focuses students on context, asking them to acknowledge the importance of time and place in shaping events. You should point out that each of the writers in this chapter and in this text (and in any text) was writing in a particular time and place. A comparison of Kingston's selection with another story, film, or television program about the Chinese would help illustrate this point. By pointing out the dreadful safety record in the mines and on the railway and the hatred and violence visited on the workers, this piece gives students a vivid contrast to the brighter picture painted by many other authors and much of the media. Comparing two portrayals is a possible topic for a follow-up discussion of the reading. Students could consider when each was written and the attitudes toward Chinese Americans at each time. How did the circumstances of time and place influence what each author produced? Was Kingston freer to complain about conditions in the past because minorities feel freer to be truthful about negative aspects of their histories in America than they did in the past? Did some whitewash history and play down the negatives to appeal to the majority or to avoid offending those in power?

Question 3 offers the students the opportunity to be creative with the facts and explore the motivation of both sides. Can anything justify the bosses' actions?

CONNIE YOUNG YU
The World of Our Grandmothers (p. 298)

Young Yu's essay, like the Seller selection in chapter 3, provides a perspective that may be unfamiliar to your students because it deals with a part of history that has been largely ignored. Both Seller and Yu explore the history of early immigrants from the perspective of immigrant women and in doing so challenge many of the stereotypical views of these women's lives. Young Yu writes the oral history of her family, especially of her grandmother, and uses it to provide a perspective on the larger community. Question 1 encourages students to do the same: write the oral history of their own grandparents. If your class is interested in oral history, this assignment can be expanded and they can use this opportunity to collect and record the oral history of a family member. Students can then share their oral histories and perhaps compare them to "official versions" of a particular time or event. For some students, recording family history can be a meaningful and memorable experience. Some students who identify as part of the mainstream believe that they don't have a unique or special family history, These students may react negatively to studying recent immigrant groups or marginalized segments of society, When these students examine their own family histories, however, they often find that their families also experienced displacement, adjustment, and hardship. This can help them relate to the course material as well as provide them with more insight into the experiences of all cultural groups that make up the population of the United States.

Questions 2 and 4 deal more directly with immigration laws. Students may need to research current immigration policy. Your class may want to use that material as the basis for further study or debate.

Question 3 invites students to write on the broad topic of tradition. Here they can relate their own family history and practice to the experiences of the Chinese family.

AMY TAN
Lindo Jong: Double Face (p. 306)

Your students may have read *The Joy Luck Club* or seen the film, and they might want to discuss either of those before reading this selection. Alternatively, if students have read Eva Hoffman, in chapter 1, they might want to review some of her concerns either before or after reading this selection. Mrs. Jong, like Hoffman, believes that there are specific characteristics that are American. Like Hoffman, she is struggling to find her place in a new culture. Questions I and 2 ask students to focus on the differences between the Chinese and the American character. Students might want to see if they agree with Mrs. Jong.

If you have students in your class whose parents are immigrants from another country, they may be able to relate to question 4. Some may feel comfortable talking about the culture clashes between immigrant parents and children raised in the United States. Of course, you wouldn't want to directly ask any student to talk about his or her own experience, but we have had many students for whom this is a current problem and they welcome a chance to share their experiences.

AMY LING
Creating One's Self: The Eaton Sisters (p. 316)

We have placed this essay at the end of the chapter because it is a critical reflection on the writing of the Eaton sisters. However, you will probably want to point out to students that Sui Sin Far, the author of "In the Land of the Free," is one of the Eaton sisters. This could lead into a general discussion of a writer's assumption of a pseudonym and when and why that is necessary. What pressures are put on writers to disguise themselves in that way? After discussing historical examples, students might consider how they respond to writing about ethnicity and gender. Do they view the pieces differently depending on the ethnicity and gender of the author? Do members of a group speak with more authority about that group? Can outsiders write about a group to which they do not belong?

The journal assignment asks students to consider the formation of their own identity and can lead to a discussion about nature vs. nurture, or about the role of culture in shaping identity.

Question 4 brings up a topic that we have noticed engages many of our students. For the last few years, our students have begun to identify themselves by their multiple heritages rather than one ethnic designation. Students might feel comfortable discussing this topic in class and talking about recent changes in outlook. Some writers have began to celebrate being "hybrid," (their term for a mixed ethnic identity). Students might want to review Sarris's description of his own mixed heritage in chapter 1.

Connecting (p. 328)

Critical Thinking and Writing

The Connecting questions relate readings to each other both within the chapter and throughout the text. For some strategies on using them in the classroom, see the comments in chapter 1 of the manual. In this set of questions, number 1 asks students to use material from the chapter to discuss a larger issue. Questions 2 through 8 raise issues dealt with in the readings in the chapter. The other questions ask students to relate the experiences of the Chinese to those of other immigrant groups.

If students have read chapter 3, they might want to look at questions 2, 8, 9, and 12, which focus on issues raised in that chapter.

Question 14 is a general question that can be answered with examples from this chapter, others, or outside information.

Though the Research questions usually require outside reading, Research question 1 might be answered with information from this text.

CHAPTER 5

AFRICAN AMERICANS: THE MIGRATION NORTH AND THE JOURNEY TOWARD CIVIL RIGHTS

The civil rights period is an important one in recent American history. During that time, many Americans bonded together to support the ideal of racial equality. Issues such as the prevalence of racism and the lack of equal opportunity were raised, and these issues are still under discussion today. Important events such as *Brown* v. *Board of Education of Topeka, Kansas*, the Montgomery bus boycott, the sit-ins and Freedom Riders led to legislation such as the Voting Rights Act of 1965 and effected profound changes in society. Schools and public facilities were desegregated, and the public at large was made aware of the brutality of racism. These events are recent enough for students to have discussed them with family members who might have participated firsthand. If your students have a lot of information about the period, they might want to begin by pooling their own knowledge about the civil rights movement. How important was it? Did it change the circumstances of their lives? Students who don't have that knowledge might ask relatives and older friends about their recollections of the period. You can assign an interview with someone who remembers the period to precede any discussion. The introduction to the chapter reviews the historical context and summarizes events. For a more dramatic introduction to the period you might want to show the first episode of the PBS series *Eyes on the Prize*. Students can use information from the introduction to the chapter and their interviews to construct a time line.

From The Constitution of South Carolina (p. 343)

This excerpt serves as a representative of the many laws that disfranchised African Americans. Such laws served to motivate many African Americans to leave their homes in the South and move north. Students may want to know what happened to these provisions and that may lead to a discussion of the Civil Rights Act and the Voting Rights Act. Emphasize the impact on people living in that part of the country of having those laws on the books for so many years. As a pre-reading question, you may want to discuss what the right to vote means both psychologically and in terms of power. After reading the excerpt, students may need to use question 1 to understand fully how South Carolina was able to nullify the Fifteenth Amendment. If you choose, look at question 2, which asks how people were disfranchised. You may want to ask students to discuss the reasons why white government wanted to take away voting rights from citizens. Students might want to discuss the Exclusion Act here.

Question 3 may lead to a broader discussion about why extra legislation was needed when we already had the Bill of Rights.

From Brown v. Board of Education of Topeka (p. 345)

Students need to be made aware that this was a landmark decision and that it paved the way for many other changes that followed. What we hoped to do by including this document was to call attention to the situation that existed in the country regarding segregation not only of schools but also of lunch counters, restrooms, and so forth. As a pre-reading activity, you might want to ask students to imagine themselves in a situation where because of some physical characteristic, such as blue eyes or blond hair, they were restricted from certain areas of the campus. How would they feel? How would they behave? How would the quality of their education change?

An alternate pre-reading activity could focus on helping students understand how important this decision was. You could introduce the *Plessy* v. *Ferguson* (1896) decision, which had permitted "separate but equal" schools. Students could discuss what the principle of "separate but equal" meant in practice. Question 2 could serve as a post-reading activity.

A copy of the Fourteenth Amendment would enhance the post-reading discussion. This could lead to a discussion about how access to education can be viewed as protection.

Questions 3 and 4 provide follow-up topics for papers or discussion.

LANGSTON HUGHES
Theme for English B (p. 347)

Students relate well to "Theme for English B" because it speaks about a situation many of them are encountering. Students may need to be told that Hughes is talking about Columbia University, and they may want to speculate about the autobiographical aspects of the poem. They also need to remember that this poem was written when restrictive laws were still on the books in the South, and even in the North, many universities had a quota system for minorities.

Question 1 focuses on the insider/outsider relationship and asks students to apply it to their own experience.

WALLACE THURMAN
From The Blacker the Berry (p. 349)

The Thurman selection is part of a chapter from a novel. In this selection, he spends considerable time letting his readers understand his heroine. The selection is unusual in that it talks about prejudice within a group, a concept that students may resist or be reluctant to acknowledge. This focus and a further discussion of the uses of irony could shape a pre-reading discussion. If time permits, you may want to show Spike Lee's film *School Daze*. The follow-up discussion might begin with a ten-minute, in-class writing assignment asking students to write a scene or a synopsis of what they think will happen next in the story.

Questions 1, 2, and 4 ask students to consider the issue of prejudice within a racial group. This point seems especially important because so many of the selections in this book deal with the prejudice individuals have had to face from members of other ethnic groups. Students can easily visualize minorities as victims of discrimination. While that is often the case, it is important for them to remember that everyone has prejudices. Sometimes individuals are prejudiced against members of their own ethnic groups because of the way these people look or behave. Of course, it is not only African Americans who are guilty of such behavior, and the class may want to contribute other examples. For instance, established immigrants may reject new immigrants from their own homelands.

Question 3 hints at the same idea but asks students to use Thurman's title to predict future events.

RALPH ELLISON
From Invisible Man (p. 358)

This reading predates the civil rights period, having been written two years before *Brown* v. *Board of Education* and ten years before the Freedom Rides, but it is included for three reasons. Ellison is an important writer, and the reading provides a background for understanding some of the difficulties African Americans faced not only in the South but in the North as well. The story personalizes the feelings that led up to the civil rights movement.

A pre-reading discussion might focus on the problems of African Americans in the North. Some students might be very well informed about the situation. Others might need you to provide additional information. You can suggest that they draw conclusions from the readings in chapter 3. What were the expectations that an African American coming from the South during the period of the Harlem Renaissance might have had about life in the North? They might also speculate about the feelings of the soldiers coming back from World War II.

Questions 1, 2, and 3 would all serve to focus post-reading discussions. They each help to establish how these mounting feelings of dispossession could result in the actions that followed in the story and ultimately throughout the nation. Students may want to look closely at the language and how often the words *ashamed, embarrassed,* and *fear* appear in the story before the narrator takes action.

If students work on question 2, they might want to follow that discussion with a discussion of question 6 in the Connecting section, which asks them to compare this excerpt with Spike Lee's film *Do the Right Thing.* Students who have seen that film might compare the causes of the escalating conflict in both pieces. What was the "'right thing" for the tenants, the crowd, and the marshals to do in this situation?

Question 4 asks students to look closely at the tone and techniques of persuasion used in both speeches. If the students have difficulty in seeing the parallels, you may want to go through Marc Antony's speech as a class, finding evidence of irony, repetition of key phrases, and so forth. Then you might have the students work in groups to find these techniques in Ellison's piece. Students can list these techniques and later use them in analyzing Dr. Martin Luther King Jr.'s letter presented later in the chapter.

ERNEST J. GAINES
From A Lesson Before Dying (p. 372)

Students may have read this book or seen the HBO movie and may want to discuss the entire work. If they are unfamiliar with the text, you might remind them that while it was written in the 1990s, it is set much earlier, during the period of segregation in the South. Students might want to review *Plessy* v. *Ferguson,* the Supreme Court's 1896 decision that upheld segregation by establishing the "separate but equal" doctrine in the nation's public schools.

The issue of authority is central to this text. The journal entry asks students to reflect on their feelings about authority figures. This could lead into a discussion of the authority relationships in the reading. How is authority designated? Does this authority figure try to put anyone at ease or does he try to maintain superiority? These questions and others should reveal the problems inherent in the classroom in the story and the difficult position the teacher is in. Question 3 asks the student to consider how language reveals the power relationship. Question 4 expands on the power relationship by asking students to think about the subliminal messages students are receiving. Students might also want to compare the power relationships between the teacher and students, between the superintendent and the teacher, and question how and why they might differ.

GWENDOLYN BROOKS
The Chicago Defender Sends a Man to Little Rock (p. 377)

The Chicago Defender Sends a Man to Little Rock provides a good example of the ways in which your own knowledge enhances your reading. Students may need more information than what is in the text to appreciate the poem about Little Rock. However, they might want to read the poem first and see what they understand without understanding the context. Students who are familiar with this history will certainly understand the poem in a different way than those who are not.

You might want to explain to the students that "New Criticism," which was popular until recently (and may have been the critical model for their high school teachers) argued that a piece of writing could stand on its own and that a reader didn't need to have any outside information about the period or the author to understand it. They can then compare that approach with the approach in this text, which proposes that without understanding the context in which something is written, understanding of the writing is diminished or impossible. This poem seems to be a strong argument for the latter principle, and the following information seems crucial to an understanding of it.

Central High School in Little Rock, Arkansas, was chosen as the only school to be integrated in the Arkansas plan to comply with *Brown* v. *Board of Education.* Nine African American students were allowed to enroll in the school in fall 1957. However, white opposition, led by Governor Orval Faubus, tried to block integration by claiming that integrating the school would result in violence, and he surrounded the school with National Guard troops to prevent integration. When the nine students tried to attend school on the second day, they were confronted by a white mob, which harassed them, and they were not able to enter the school. The courts ordered Faubus to remove the National Guard, but mobs of whites prevented the African American children from attending school. The school did not become integrated until President Eisenhower sent in federal troops. The *Chicago Defender* is a large, important African American newspaper. Four African American journalists went to Central High School on September 23 to report on the reception of the African American students. They were mistaken by the mob for parents escorting their children to school and were chased and attacked.

The poem carries through the themes of King and Farmer when they discuss the "mob mentality" and the irony of the evil that exists in these seemingly normal societies. Question 1 can be used as a pre-reading activity and questions 2, 3, and 4 can be used to focus a post-reading discussion.

JAMES FARMER
"Tomorrow Is for Our Martyrs" (p. 380)

Farmer is an important leader in the fight for civil rights who may be unfamiliar to students. Have them review CORE (in the introduction to the chapter and the headnote) and recognize its importance. This selection from Farmer's autobiography discusses the murder of three civil rights workers (Schwerner, Chaney, and Goodman) who had gone to Mississippi as part of a large-scale voter registration drive aimed at registering African Americans to vote. This movement was met with resistance from local communities. This reading helps to present some of the complexities of the civil rights period as well as to relate some of the dangers that faced civil rights activists.

You may find that your students have trouble comprehending such overt racism and community-supported violence in the United States. Some students know about these events or have seen the film *Mississippi Burning.* Otherwise, you might want to show the film. You may want to review the situation that existed in the South before reading the selection. Such a review might help students set the scene and recognize the danger to the three men and the fear and hostility in the southern white communities. However, if you do show the film, you and the students need to be aware of the criticism it received from the African American community because it elevated the role of the white FBI agents and neglected the role African Americans played. The version of events in the reading can be compared to the version in the film.

Questions 1, 2, and 3 can provide topics for post-reading discussions. Question 3 may require some background on nonviolence. You might want to have students read "Letter from Birmingham Jail" at this time.

If you want to focus on the complexities of the period, you can review the political situation. What was at stake for whites if more African Americans had the ability to vote and were generally integrated into the community? What was at stake for African Americans if the power base changed in their favor? Have students refer to the introduction to the chapter and other sources to fill in the context.

You might want to ask students what would inspire members of the power group to assist the oppressed and vice versa. If you choose, this approach, questions 2, 3, and 4 can focus discussion and be used as writing topics.

MARTIN LUTHER KING JR.
Letter from Birmingham Jail (p. 389)

This piece is a classic, and students may have read it previously. But, students can gain fresh insights by reading it within the context of the other readings in this chapter and text. We have included it because it so well defines King's position on nonviolence and because the writing is so powerful in its ability to defend, persuade, and move. The author's note at the beginning of the reading helps set the context.

If you choose to focus on King's purpose in writing the letter, you may want to have students speculate, using the introduction or their own knowledge, on what these clergymen may have written about King's activities to elicit such a long letter in response. As the students read, have them pay special attention to the issues King brings up and how he defends his activities and persuades his readers to join him.

An understanding of King's position on nonviolence is essential to a solid understanding of the civil rights period. As a pre-reading activity, you may want to discuss the whole concept of "turning the other cheek" and what can be gained from such an approach. You can have students take a stand on whether or not they advocate nonviolence. After reading the selection, they can see where they agree or disagree with King. Since a selection from Malcolm X that presents his viewpoint on the nonviolence question follows, you may want to have students compare the two men's philosophies. If *Do the Right Thing* has been discussed or shown in your class, you might point out that Lee ends the film with quotations from both King and Malcolm X about violence as a solution to problems. Why did he end the film with quotations from both men that express opposing points of view?

One other approach you and your class may wish to take with this reading is to look at the ironies of the situation. As your students know about the period from the introduction and other selections, you may want to ask them to assemble lists of the crimes committed by whites against African Americans during this period—murder, destruction of property, obstruction of the right to vote, and so forth. In some cases, even the clergy were involved, as we see in Farmer's selection. With this background, students can put King's "crime" into perspective. They may also want to address the question of whether or not he was just exercising his right of freedom to assemble. Questions 2 and 3 can then be used to focus the post-reading discussion. Students can use the essay topics in questions 3 and 4 to evaluate for themselves how successful King was in his arguments.

For a different perspective on King, read Septima Clark's *Ready from Within*. This book, which is primarily the story of literacy work in several African American communities during this period, presents a candid portrait of King.

MALCOLM X
From The Autobiography of Malcolm X (p. 403)

Given the success of Spike Lee's *Malcolm X*, you will probably find that students know a great deal about this leader of the black separatist movement. Students might enjoy seeing the film again and remembering that Malcolm taught himself to read in prison by going through the dictionary and working his way through the library alphabetically. Students may also be interested in reviewing the changes in philosophy that emerged later in his career. We chose this particular selection because it represents Malcolm X's position on nonviolence. Make sure students understand that position as well as his position on Christianity in general. Then ask students to compare it to King's and other advocates of nonviolent solutions to problems.

After reading, you can follow up with question 1, which asks students to articulate Malcolm X's position on nonviolence and the appropriate use of violence. This can be used as the basis for a debate between those supporting King's position and those supporting Malcolm's. You might choose Malcolm as an example of someone who rises above the hardships of his upbringing. What motivated him to overcome the obstacles that society placed in his path?

A peripheral issue raised by question 3 is whether the rhetoric of Malcolm X and many of the other leaders of the civil rights movement focuses exclusively on men. If you do choose to pursue this topic, you might consider the role of women in the movement. Women leaders were not very visible. Rosa Parks, of course, was important but was not part of the power structure. Coretta King did not become a leader of the movement until after her husband's death. If women were excluded from leadership, was that a factor of the period (pre-women's movement), or was it the result of the attitudes of the male leaders? Were women active in other civil rights movements, such as the organizations for migrant workers or the Red Power movement? For additional information on women's roles in the civil rights movement, see Clark's *Ready from Within*. Question 2 in the Research questions at the end of the chapter also deals with this issue.

MARY HELEN WASHINGTON
The Darkened Eye Restored (p. 410)

This selection is a work of literary criticism. Students might want to discuss how it differs from the other readings in the chapter. Before discussion, you might want students to do the group assignment because it asks them to define many of the terms Washington uses.

The text discusses the role of women in the literary tradition. Students might want to discuss the influence of the gender and ethnicity of an author on them as readers. Then they might want to broaden that discussion to consider whether groups have traditionally been excluded from participation in the arts or in certain arts because of gender or ethnicity. If students have read chapter 4, particularly the essay about the Eaton sisters, they might want to reconsider the use of pseudonyms for authors (for a more extensive discussion of this issue see *Creating One's Self: The Eaton Sisters* in chapter 4, Instructor's Resource Manual). Students can write on this subject by answering question 3, or if they want to deal with it in light of recent honors for African American woman writers, they can answer question 4.

Connecting (p. 423)

Critical Thinking and Writing

The Connecting questions can be used to bring students up to date and help them assess the effects of the civil rights movement on the various branches of government and on the public. Questions 3, 4, 6, 7, and 8 focus on those issues. Questions to discuss include a consideration of what lasting effects the civil rights movement had and the changes that are still being resisted. Students may want to look at the time line constructed during the Beginning exercise to evaluate what was truly lasting and what was superficial. Students can review the lengths the South went to in order to keep African Americans from voting and having a say in legislation, the sacrifices made to gain those rights, and the difficulties in changing attitudes. Some students may feel that things have not changed a great deal since the 1960s in spite of new legislation. They may charge that racism still exists in this country. Related issues involve affirmative action and equal opportunity.

Another approach would be to have students look at civil rights laws and discuss how successfully they feel the legislation has been in changing actual attitudes (see question 2). In order to do this, students would have to understand the laws, and you may have to provide them with copies or summaries of the laws. An alternative would be for them to investigate affirmative action programs on their own campuses. They could interview administrators to discover the rationale behind the programs and how they are implemented. Knowing the problems African Americans had in the past getting education, jobs, and housing should make students at least understand some of the thinking about affirmative action programs. Students might want to read Richard Rodriguez, who is an opponent of affirmative action.

Question 9 asks students to make comparisons between African Americans' struggles and those of other groups. Questions 10 through 12 ask them to consider broader issues. The Research questions focus specifically on women, civil rights leaders, and the history of civil disobedience. These might be modified into topics for shorter papers.

CHAPTER 6

PUERTO RICANS: THE VIEW FROM THE MAINLAND

This chapter covers a wider time span than many of the others. We decided on the broader scope because the history of Puerto Ricans in the United States is a long and varied one. The introduction, which students should read before reading the selections, covers the history of the island's relationship with the mainland. It should give students enough background material to allow them to complete the Beginning exercise, which asks them to speculate about Puerto Ricans' reasons for emigrating. If there are Puerto Rican students in your class, they can lead the discussion.

Following the discussion, students can compare the situation of Puerto Ricans with those of other earlier and later immigrants. Early Puerto Rican immigrants were arriving at the same time as the big influx of immigrants from Europe. Students might consider how their situations were different: for example, Puerto Ricans were American citizens and had exposure to the English language in Puerto Rico. A question students might want to tackle is whether or not Puerto Rican immigrants have an easier time than other immigrants.

From The Foraker Act (p. 437)

We included this excerpt from the Foraker Act to point up the limits to Puerto Rican independence that were in place at the turn of the century. The act placed Puerto Rico under the jurisdiction of a presidentially appointed military governor and a council with an American majority. It also designated English as the official language. In a pre-reading discussion, you may want to point out that Puerto Rico was self-governing prior to being ceded to the United States. As the introduction to the chapter points out, the Puerto Rican people had worked hard to win this right from the Spanish Crown.

The questions ask students to focus on specifics in the act that point up the lack of independence Puerto Ricans actually had. This helps explain the interest of early immigrants in politics.

Question 2 asks students to consider the power structure in Puerto Rico. Is there anything ironic about the United States having this type of power over a territory?

JESUS COLON
Kipling and I (p. 438)

This selections comes from the book *A Puerto Rican in New York* and recounts one of Colón's experiences in coming to and adjusting to America. A pre-reading activity might deal with the expectations of European immigrants like Panunzio in chapter 3, who arrived during the same period as Colón, and the expectations of Puerto Ricans. Would they differ, and if so, how? As students read the selections, they can think about whether or not Colón's expectations were met. Students might enjoy reading the Kipling poem "If—" before and after they read Colón. Students could think about Kipling, his audience, and the advice a father in his world could give his son. What would that son's expectations be? How would they differ from Colón's? Could that poem be relevant to a black Puerto Rican living in New York City in the early 1900s? The irony of the situation should make a good post-reading discussion topic. Question 1 may be helpful in discussing Colón's success, or lack of success, in meeting his expectations. Question 4, dealing with the burning of the poem at the end of "Kipling and I" may add depth to your discussion.

Since the issue of power relationships is also a strong theme in this selection, as a pre-reading activity it may be helpful for the students to review the social and political situation at the time this piece was written. Where would a black Puerto Rican fit in the power structure in the 1900s? Students can look at the Foraker Act, which defines the power relationships between the United States and Puerto Rico. Alternately, this discussion may focus on the college and even your own classroom. Question 3 encourages students to discuss this aspect of Colón's work and could be used to structure a follow-up discussion.

PIRI THOMAS
Puerto Rican Paradise (p. 443)

This reading focuses on Thomas's mother's nostalgia for Puerto Rico. A pre-reading activity might involve discussing the reasons why the past often seems better than the present. Students can share stories their parents have told of the "good old days." Questions 1, 2, and 3 can be used to begin follow-up discussions. Another aspect of the story that might be explored is the happy family Thomas describes. Pre-reading questions might include Do you need money to be happy? What makes a family happy? Students could be asked to write for ten minutes about a particularly happy moment for their families, explaining why it was so satisfying.

Question 4 brings up a serious controversy: Do you need to be a member of a group to understand the experience of that group? This discussion might expand to include the following questions: Who should write about the experience of minorities? Who should teach ethnic courses or ethnic material? What is the role of the white teacher and the ethnic student when discussing ethnic material? What is the importance of books such as this one, where the focus is on letting ethnic groups speak for themselves? See Hughes's poem "Theme for English B" in chapter 5.

For a different picture of a family experiencing poverty, see Yezierska in chapter 3.

NICHOLASA MOHR
The English Lesson (p. 448)

This story makes use of multiple points of view to contrast the expectations of the ESL teacher and those of her adult students. Both teacher and students experience a learning opportunity. Your students might want to discuss the role of teachers and students in general. Who does the teaching and learning in a classroom? Is it only one-sided? The image of a teacher learning from her students may be a new one for your students to consider. However, that realization, that teachers are also learners, may help dispel some long-held classroom myths, that the teacher has all the power and authority and that the teacher is the dispenser of all knowledge. Such a realignment of power also should help students become aware of their own responsibility for their education.

An important feature of this story is the multiple perspective that it presents. The journal entry allows students to write from the perspective of one of the characters. The group assignment asks students to identify all of the different participants in the story and discuss their perspectives on each other and the teacher. This assignment leads into the essay questions that reflect on the question of equal treatment and opportunity for everyone in America. Students may want to relate this story to some of the readings in chapter 1, especially Adams. What does this story have to say about recent immigrants and the American Dream?

JUDITH ORTIZ COFER
From **The Line of the Sun** (p. 460)

Marisol, like Piri Thomas's mother, idealizes life in Puerto Rico. A pre-reading question might ask students to imagine what their lives might have been like if they had been born in a different time and place. Students could also question why someone would want to change the time or place of their birth. Marisol, like many of the other characters in this text, and like many students we find in our classrooms, is caught "halfway between cultures." This can be a very uncomfortable position, and its difficulties should be discussed either before or after reading the selection. Question 4 focuses on the bicultural issue. Students might not understand or be sympathetic to her dissatisfaction with life in the United States. If this is the case, question 3 calls on students to look back at the text and speculate. As the question suggests, Marisol uses visions of Puerto Rico to help her escape from current problems. Students might discuss the effectiveness of this strategy and relate it to their own behavior.

Questions 1 and 2 discuss Marisol's relationship with her mother. The problems of wanting to fit in when you are an outsider (Marisol's views of herself in school) and of being ashamed of immigrant parents might be shared by some students. Others may not understand why it bothers Marisol to have a mother who is "exotic." A discussion of her attitudes could bring up these different points of view. Asking students to write for ten minutes about whether they feel Marisol's reaction to her mother's visit to school was appropriate or mature could precede the discussion.

MARTIN ESPADA
Mrs. Baez Serves Coffee on the Third Floor (p. 467)

This poem is very visual and offers opportunities for students to create their own visual representations. Students could begin their response by drawing a specific place, person, or event depicted in the poem or they might want to freewrite a response to the emotional content. Then they could move forward with question 2, which asks them to list the images that give the poem its power. Question 2 might be preceded by an oral reading of the poem in class. Then the groups can translate the poetry into prose. Questions 3 and 4 ask students to write from the perspective of the various characters and is a good opportunity to understand and discuss the difference your position makes to your reaction to an event or a set of circumstances. A follow-up discussion could address the effect on individuals of living amid urban decay and the ways in which they work to maintain their dignity in spite of circumstances.

LINDA CHAVEZ
No to Puerto Rican Statehood (p. 470)

Chavez opposes Puerto Rican statehood. She, unlike Ferre, who was born in Puerto Rico, has not lived there. Students might want to discuss whether or not this fact influences her credibility. Can she really understand the situation for Puerto Ricans when she isn't one of them? On the other hand, perhaps Ferre is too close to the issue and can't be objective. The readings seem to present a different picture of Puerto Rico. How do students account for these differences?

If you wish your students to debate the issue of Puerto Rican statehood, you might want them to do the group assignment that asks them to list the arguments for and against statehood.

ROSARIO FERRE
Puerto Rico, U.S.A. (p. 473)

This essay can be read together with the piece by Linda Chavez. Both respond to questions concerning Puerto Rican statehood. Ferre supports statehood, while Chavez does not. After students have read both pieces, and perhaps done some additional research, you might want to have them debate the issue.

The questions are designed to help students research and understand the geography, economy, history, and society of Puerto Rico. Some of your students may be very familiar with the relationship between Puerto Rico and the United States. Hopefully, you can use them as resources to enlighten other students. If students have access to the Internet, they can easily familiarize themselves with the background information they need to understand these pieces.

Question 4 brings up a controversial issue, not only for Puerto Rico, but for other parts of the United States as well. Students may be interested in researching and discussing the English Only movement and thinking about whether it should apply in a place such as Puerto Rico, or if it should apply anywhere.

Connecting (p. 476)

Critical Thinking and Writing

Like the other sets of Connecting questions, these attempt to have students see the relation between the experiences of one writer and another, one group and another. Questions 1, 2, and 3 specifically ask students to support their points with examples from within the chapter. The other questions point up relationships across chapters.

When dealing with the more general questions, students are always encouraged to use specific examples, but these examples can come from other sources as well as their own experience. However, the Research questions require information from outside sources. For general suggestions about the ways to use the Connecting questions, see the remarks in part 1, Connecting.

CHAPTER 7

JAPANESE AMERICANS: IN CAMP, IN COMMUNITY

This chapter centers on the experience of Japanese Americans during their internment by the United States government in World War II. The Japanese have had a long history in the United States and have certainly contributed to our society in many other periods besides the internment one. However, we have chosen to focus on that period for two reasons: (1) We believe that Japanese Americans suffered a terrible wrong when they were interned. Many students are not aware of this important and shameful period in American history. (2) The internment experience for Japanese Americans (like the Holocaust for many Jews) has generated a great deal of eloquent writing. The readings in this chapter are very interrelated; they all deal with one very specific incident.

You might use the Beginning Pre-reading Writing Exercise before the introduction is read. It asks students to imagine themselves in the situation that faced many of the Japanese and Japanese Americans on the West Coast. They were suddenly told they must leave their homes and were just as bewildered as the students will be doing this exercise. If the students question the order to leave, your answer can be that in this make-believe world the law orders them to do so. Part of the follow-up discussion could address their feelings of confusion. Students might also want to talk about what they would most regret leaving behind. Then, when they read the introduction, they may be able to empathize more with the Japanese and Japanese Americans.

Japanese Relocation Order (p. 488)

This executive order gave the secretary of war the power to evacuate from specific military areas any residents who were considered risks to national security. Legal documents are dense, and sometimes their implications are not clear. In this case, no specific ethnic group was mentioned, yet the order was applied almost exclusively to Japanese Americans. How do the students account for that? Is that provision in the document itself? After reading the order, you may want to look at questions 1 and 2, which require them to reread the order carefully. They might compare the document to the Chinese Exclusion Act in chapter 4 or to the grandfather clauses in some southern states' constitutions that disfranchised African Americans (see chapter 5, Introduction). This can open a discussion on the ability of lawmakers to use words to disguise their purpose rather than state it. It can also call into question the ability of the Bill of Rights, in chapter 3, and the Constitution to protect citizens and guarantee their rights.

Question 3 asks students to analyze the order's impact on the civil rights of citizens. This requires much more thought and is a theme that recurs throughout the section. Students might want to wait to tackle it in writing after they have read more. During discussion, try to get them to think about whether or not and under what conditions such an occurrence could happen again.

MONICA SONE
Pearl Harbor Echoes in Seattle (p. 490)

Sone's autobiography is a good place to begin reading because she repeats some of the legal and historical background already presented in the introduction. Additionally, her story is engrossing. Readers are able to see the effects of the Internment Act on a real family. The introduction and the Internment Act serve as pre-reading for this selection. The Yamamoto reading provides a natural sequel, and the two might be read together.

After seeing the practical effects of the Internment Act, students may feel better prepared to answer question 4, which is similar to question 3 in the Responding questions that follow the Japanese Relocation Order. This is an important issue and should be dealt with at some point.

By asking students to use a letter format, question 1 will help them visualize an audience other than the teacher and help them learn to write for different audiences and purposes.

Question 2 or 3 could be used to structure post-reading activities. The resulting outline or list of attitudes could be the topic of a whole-class discussion. For question 3, students could also compare these attitudes and reactions of a real family with the stereotype from which the government was supposedly protecting itself.

JOHN OKADA
From No-no Boy (p. 502)

This excerpt from the novel tells the story of a Japanese American who refused to enlist in the American army and at war's end must face others who made different choices. In this case, his situation is further complicated by the attitude of his mother and his own feelings of being torn between two loyalties and two identities. A pre-reading discussion might explain his situation and ask students what they think they would do if they were caught in this bind. Alternately, students could be asked how they determine their loyalties.

Question 4 deals with the issue of dual identity, a theme that recurs throughout this book. Mora deals with it directly in "Elena" in Chapter 8. Many students may experience conflicts between their culture and mainstream American culture. We often see students whose loyalty to their language and culture makes even the task of learning English an act of betrayal. For them, going to college can mean turning their backs on the family, who can't understand their ambitions or the changes that take place. Your students may want to answer question 1, which would allow them to discuss their personal resolution of this problem.

Question 3 could be used as a ten-minute, in-class, writing assignment designed to begin discussion of the story. Question 2 might also serve as the basis for a small-group or whole-class post-reading discussion.

HISAYE YAMAMOTO
The Legend of Miss Sasagawara (p. 514)

The Yamamoto selection takes the reader into a camp such as the one in which the Sone family was interned. Students can then understand more clearly what happened to the Sones and the thousands of Japanese Americans who were interned. For a sensitive person like Miss Sasagawara, the effect was devastating.

As a pre-reading activity you might ask students some of the following questions: What do you imagine the camps were like? What do they think internees most missed? Describe the camps. Students can use information from the introduction and their own knowledge to imagine what life was like in the camps. Their speculations can then be checked against the description of the camp in the reading. Questions 1 and 2 could be used as the basis for small-group or whole-class post-reading discussions. Students might be given ten minutes to draw the camp and then asked to share these drawings with the class.

You can focus on what each student chose to draw and why that image was especially significant. You might want to expand the discussion to include the methods your students would have used for coping.

Another possible topic for discussion would be the internees' attitude toward America. As either a pre- or post-reading activity, students can discuss what might motivate the different reactions and even what they think their own reactions might have been. This is a good place to mention the many Japanese Americans who volunteered to serve in the armed forces. You should also acknowledge, however, that there were Japanese whose loyalty shifted to Japan (see *No-no Boy*). Where do they think the Sone family's loyalties would he?

Question 4 calls for more interpretive skills. If you want students to write this essay, some class discussion of the literary devices in the story would be helpful. The eightfold path is a Buddhist doctrine based on the incontrovertibility of human suffering. In order to escape from being controlled by the "body-identified mind," correct false values, and eliminate suffering, you must follow right views, purpose, speech, conduct, means of livelihood, effort, kinds of awareness or mind control, and concentration or meditation (Ross, *Three Ways of Asian Wisdom*, Simon and Schuster, 1966).

Students might also want to compare the attitude of Miss Sasagawara's father toward the Internment with Kubota's response in Hongo's "Kubota" or the reaction of the Japanese Americans Takaki describes in "Roots." Both of these readings are found in Chapter 7.

LAWSON FUSAO INADA
Concentration Constellation (p. 527)

This poem presents the Western landscape as a constellation of internment camps, a perspective that may be unusual for your students but one that illustrates how events can change the perception of a place or a time. It demonstrates the way artists can use collective experience to create works of art and literature. It also reflects the lingering effect of the Internment on Japanese Americans.

Question 2 encourages students to re-create the pattern the camps make on a map. The follow-up discussion can bring up the reaction of the local population in the vicinity of the camps. Some topics that might be raised involve the way students think they might have reacted if an internment camp was located in their part of the country, their response if they have ever visited one of the camps or been near a camp site, or the reaction of family or anyone they have known who was interned.

The title suggests that readers should think of the camp as a concentration camp rather than an internment camp. Students can discuss the difference that designation makes in their perception. They might want to compare the Japanese American internment to Rosa's World War II experiences. If you compare Japanese American internment to the treatment of Jews by Nazi Germany, however, be prepared to deal with some touchy issues: Were the American camps as brutal as the German? Why didn't the American population object to the camps? Some Jewish students may feel that comparing the situations diminishes the horror of the Holocaust, and their feelings need to be acknowledged. Japanese American victims also need their sacrifices and hardships validated.

A choral reading of the poem adds to its power. Let students organize the readings, assign the parts, and so forth. Then, as a post-reading activity, they can discuss the reasons for their choices and try out other options.

GARRETT HONGO
Kubota (p. 529)

This touching story is another examination (with "The Legend of Miss Sasagawara" and "Roots") of the issue of silence and the Japanese American response to the Internment. Many victims responded to the situation by feeling ashamed of themselves rather than angry at the government and reacted by being silent about their treatment. Question 4 deals directly with this issue.

Question 2 raises awareness of the treatment of historical events in school texts by asking students to reflect on their own histories. A follow-up discussion could ask students if they feel the Internment and other unpleasant episodes in American history should be dealt with more completely in history classes. They might want to discuss how other countries report events that don't show their country in a favorable light. Students might research the presentation of the Holocaust in German schools. Films such as *The Nasty Girl* indicate that many Germans want to forget the events of World War II.

DICK THORNBURGH
Making Amends (p. 538)

You might want students to read this speech along with the newspaper article that follows it. Students could then write a letter from Korematsu to Thornburgh responding to his address. Then Thornburgh could answer. You could also set this up as a dialogue between pairs of students, one taking the role of Korematsu and one of Thornburgh.

Your students may not know much about the struggle for reparations and an apology that Japanese Americans have gone through. They might want to look through the Takaki selection to understand why it took Japanese Americans so long to seek reparations.

Question 3 brings up a larger issue. Should the American government pay reparations to other groups that have suffered injustice at its hands? Students may want to discuss or debate this issue before writing about it. At the same time, they can discuss question 4, which asks how important it is for a government to acknowledge its acts of injustice toward its citizens. Students may need to be reminded that American citizens of Japanese descent were interned along with Japanese nationals.

BOB POOL
Uncovering Internment Papers (p. 539)

This recent news story presents significant and disturbing evidence that the authorities incarcerated Japanese Americans because of their race and then lied about it to the Supreme Court. Students may want to discuss this duplicity of the government. Since we live in a time when many citizens are cynical about government ethics you might want to broaden this discussion to include other examples of government corruption and racism. Students may want to consider how much decisions by the government have been based on racism and presented to the public as instances of protecting national security. This can serve as pre-writing for question 3. Students might want to consider whether a history teacher has a responsibility to present the most comprehensive view of history, even if it is unflattering to the government.

Another important point that is raised by this piece is the protection of civil liberties. After students have completed their journal entries, they may want to have a whole-class discussion based on their responses.

RONALD TAKAKI
Roots (p. 542)

This reading also views the internment experience from today's perspective. Takaki encourages Japanese Americans to join him and break their silence about their experience. This silence, which is the traditional Japanese way of dealing with hardship, has not allowed them to find release from the sense of shame and guilt that the Internment produced. A pre-reading discussion might focus on question 2. This could lead to a discussion of the guilt feelings of victims, or students could speculate about the attitudes of Japanese Americans today. Have they forgotten the Internment? Do they tell their children and grandchildren about it? What attitude do they have? What about reparations? Why did it take so long for the U.S. government to begin to make amends? Answers to these questions can function as pre-writing for the essay topic of question 4.

In order to answer question 3, students may need to gather more information about Japanese culture. Japanese or Japanese American students or an Asian language and literature department would be good resources. Some inferences can be made from the introduction to the chapter and the readings themselves.

Question 1 asks students to consider once again the names of groups. Students are often unaware that *Oriental* is a pejorative term. A frank discussion about the use of names and sensitivity to the feelings of members of ethnic groups would be appropriate here. You might begin by asking students if anyone has ever called them names and how they feel when that happens. They can then discuss appropriate reactions. If the class is not comfortable with controversial issues, you might ask them to consider the effect being called names has on children. This will make the discussion less personally threatening and perhaps more comfortable.

Connecting (p. 547)

Critical Thinking and Writing

You might choose to use questions 1 and 11 in this set as the basis for discussion, debate, or as the topic for a formal paper after students have read the entire chapter since the questions deal with issues that are central motivation for the Internment and reparations. Although after reading the chapter students should have enough information for discussion, you might want to suggest some additional outside reading.

The other questions vary in focus. Questions 2 and 3 ask students to discuss readings within the chapter. Questions 5 through 10 ask students to consider specific connections to other parts of the text.

Questions 4, 5, 6, and 7 ask students to use material from the text to support their points about broad issues. Question 8 asks for a personal response.

The Research questions in this section ask for specific answers to questions. Students might want to work on scaled-down versions of these questions, or you might want to introduce them as discussion topics in class.

CHAPTER 8

CHICANOS: NEGOTIATING POLITICAL AND CULTURAL BOUNDARIES

This chapter chronicles some of the experiences of Chicanos in the United States. Students need to read the introduction to the chapter in order to understand the long history of Mexicans in the Southwest. Chicanos are defined as people of Mexican descent born and raised in the United States. While some of the characters in the stories are Mexican migrant workers or Mexican nationals, their children are Chicano. As is the case in all of the chapters, we hope that the readings present enough of a range of characters, attitudes, and behaviors that students will rethink any stereotypical ideas they have of groups. Again, one of the challenges for a text such as this one is to try to represent cultures without creating stereotypes. Here we want students to appreciate the importance Mexican culture plays in the lives of Chicanos (and the influence it has in the United States in general) without reinforcing any typical stereotypes.

The Beginning Pre-Reading/Writing exercise was designed to make students aware of the feelings that Mexicans might have had when they found themselves suddenly living in another country with a different dominant language and culture. After students share their own feelings, they could speculate about the experiences of both Mexicans and Americans living in a time of changing borders.

From The Treaty of Guadalupe Hidalgo (p. 560)

This excerpt is interesting because of the promises it makes and because it illustrates the changes forced on the Mexican people living in the ceded areas. The article in the treaty guaranteeing Mexican citizens their rights to property, religion, and liberty was never passed by Congress. You might want to have students compare this treaty to the broken promises in the treaties between the United States and American Indians (see Deloria and Lytle in Chapter 2).

Question 1 asks students to put themselves in the place of people living in the region. Question 2 tries to make students aware of the history of the Southwest. Some students may not know that during the period of the westward movement Mexican settlers predated Europeans and were the majority in much of the Southwest, Texas, and California. Have students review the introduction to the chapter as pre-writing and use outside sources if necessary.

Question 4 might be used to begin the post-reading discussion. You could ask students how they would feel if they suddenly found they were living in a place that had been taken over by a neighboring country. What would their concerns be?

CESAR CHAVEZ
The Organizer's Tale (p. 566)

This reading and the story and poem that follow all talk about the experiences of migrant workers. This is an important aspect of Chicano history since many Mexicans came to the United States as migrant workers. An effective way to introduce the situation of these people would be to show the Edward R. Murrow video *Harvest of Shame.* You might begin by asking students what they know about the food they eat. Do they understand that some crops have to be harvested by hand and how difficult that work is? Students who have read John Steinbeck's *Grapes of Wrath* or seen the film might be able to bring it into the discussion.

Before students read "The Organizer's Tale," they might find it helpful to review the events of the McCarthy era. Some students may have little knowledge of this period, and this additional information can make them more aware of the risks that Chávez and his fellow workers were taking when they decided to fight for their rights. As a post-reading activity, you may want to follow up with question 2.

Another alternative that you may want to pursue would be to look at the way in which Chávez's organization developed. Following a general discussion about the plight of the migrant worker, you may want to ask students to list the things that they would consider changing first if they were to live and work under the conditions of the migrant workers. After reading the selection, students can examine the way Chávez approached this problem by looking at questions 1, 3, and 4.

Question 1 could also be used to focus follow-up activities. Working individually or in a group, students could isolate the specific techniques Chávez learned.

Question 4 can be answered adequately from material in the essay, but it would be helpful to have students do some outside reading. It is important for students to understand the consequences of Chávez and the United Farm Workers. Current issues for the union include concerns over pesticides and other cancer-causing additives.

TOMAS RIVERA
Christmas Eve/La Noche Buena (p. 575)

This selection has been reprinted in both Spanish and English because the story was originally written in Spanish and the English version is a translation. Having a bilingual text makes the work accessible to speakers of both languages and validates each. For readers of both languages, the side-by-side text adds enrichment. Students who read Spanish should enjoy the opportunity to read the story in the language in which it was written. The story brings up a recurring theme in this text: the difficulties individuals face when they are in an alien culture or when they feel unable to deal with circumstances. For a post-reading activity, students might compare doña María's reactions to Beret's in Rölvaag's "Facing the Great Desolation" in chapter 3. Doña María and Beret are two of the women characters in the text who become overwhelmed by the challenge of adjustment to a new world. They can be compared to the many women who do. See Cisneros and Limón in this chapter.

Students may clarify their own responses to the text by looking at question 3 and writing a ten-minute, in-class response to the story discussing Rivera's and their own attitude toward doña

María. Where do their sympathies lie and why? They can then share their responses with the class. Question 1 may work well as a follow-up to this discussion.

Another aspect of this story is the way society looks at people who have difficulty in fitting in. Do they tend to make it easier for outsiders to become part of the mainstream, or do they inhibit them? Question 4 could be used to initiate this topic. A class discussion of the various points of view of the onlookers will help students understand the ways in which economic, cultural, and political issues can affect your viewpoint.

PAT MORA
Elena (p. 586)

"Elena" deals with the problems of being bilingual and bicultural. "Elena" sees these issues from the recent immigrant's point of view, wrestling with the changes that are taking place in the speaker's children and her conflict with her husband. You may have students in your class who are living through these cultural conflicts and may wish to write or speak about them. Question 4 invites them to report on their own experience. Students might want to refer to Hoffman in chapter 1 and compare her experiences to Elena's. What is different about Hoffman's situation?

ARTURO ISLAS
From Migrant Souls (p. 587)

This selection from a recent novel brings up issues of prejudice that reflect current concerns in American society: defining the physical and psychological border between the United States and Mexico, racial prejudice within a group toward members who possess characteristics such as skin color, language, or behavior that fit the mainstream's stereotype of that group, racial prejudice by the majority, who want to restrict members of the group by limiting their entry into the country or their opportunities for jobs and housing. To understand more fully the situation of Mexican Americans living on the border and what they must face when they try to cross into what was once their homeland or is the home of relatives, students can review the history of the border discussed in the introduction to the chapter. It is important for them to understand that for many Mexicans and Mexican Americans, the border is an arbitrary line.

This reading, like others in the text, openly acknowledges the existence of prejudice within a racial group. Because all racial groups have such prejudice, you may want to have a pre-reading discussion about these feelings and perhaps speculate on how they come about.

Islas also tackles the issue of names and their power to distort thinking and inflict pain. This echoes many of the concerns of the civil rights period. Students might want to review Gates in chapter 1. These are current concerns for many groups. Takaki in chapter 7 discusses how the issue relates to the Japanese American.

If students want to discuss prejudice from without and its effects, they can refer to question 1, which asks them to consider the effects of the deportation stories on children who live on the border. Some may also have been raised with stories like these or with stories that evoked other fears such as fear of different ethnic groups. Students may feel comfortable discussing those fears. If they do not, this might be a good entrée into a discussion of the mistrust and fear that often poisons relations among people.

Any of these issues may be used to begin the pre-reading or post-reading discussion. However, the piece also has a humorous side, which students may want to discuss; question 3 offers a suitable post-reading activity.

SANDRA CISNEROS
Woman Hollering Creek (p. 596)

Here is a reading that deals with women in a difficult situation. Before students read it, you might review with them some of the other women characters they have encountered in the text, particularly in this chapter. A more detailed discussion might follow the reading.

We felt that Cisneros led us to believe that the story would have a negative ending, and we were pleased with the turn of events. The story presents a too familiar situation, a woman far from family and friends, that usually has a very unhappy ending. But this woman acts.

A pre-reading discussion might ask students to define women's roles in various cultures. What are the responsibilities of a wife and mother? Which responsibility is primary? What are the responsibilities of a husband? What should a woman do if she is abused or mistreated by her husband?

The post-reading activities might begin with students writing for ten minutes in class about their response to Cleófilas's actions. Was she right to leave? What might have happened if she had stayed? This might lead to a discussion of different images and role models for women, for example, women like Felice. Any of the four questions would work well as a follow-up to the writing, but question 2 specifically asks them to consider Cleófilas's options.

Students might enjoy writing a different ending for the story (question 4). They could write the ending individually or in a group, as a story or as a scene between any of the characters. They could then read these aloud in class and compare them to the original ending.

GRACIELA LIMON
From The Memories of Ana Calderón (p. 606)

This selection introduces students to the life of a migrant worker. At the same time, it examines the ways in which gender expectations can determine the role one is asked to play in the family.

Questions 1, 2, and 4 focus on working conditions for migrant farmworkers. Students might want to discuss how such conditions motivated a man like César Chávez to found the United Farm Workers Union. You may have students who may themselves or whose parents have been migrant workers. They might be willing to share this information during class discussion. Because the selection is so short, students may need to do outside research to really understand the conditions of migrant workers.

Questions 3 focuses on gender issues. As a pre-writing exercise, you might ask students to write about the gender roles and expectations within their own families and then share that information with the class. Some might be able to relate to Ana's situation. Your students may have the same conflicts as Ana has and may benefit from discussing them.

RUBEN SALAZAR
From Border Correspondent (p. 610)

Students might want to discuss the tragedy of Ruben Salazar's death at the hands of Los Angeles County sheriffs while covering the Chicano Moratorium demonstration. They might use the Internet to find out more details about the Chicano Moratorium and Salazar's death. This research would lead into question 2, the group research and discussion about the political and social climate at the time. After students reflect on the term *Chicano*, they might want to do the journal entry that asks them to identify and label their own ethnic identity. The might want to refer to the Gates selection in chapter 1 that discusses labeling African Americans. A side issue that may come up for discussion is labeling itself. Do they feel that they can label their ethnic identity, or is it too complex to be described under one term? What do the labels mean anyway? You may want to discuss the evolution of names for people from Spanish-speaking countries and the political ramifications of those names.

Question 3 asks students to use the information from this discussion in order to elaborate on Salazar's definition of *Chicano.*

Question 4 raises a familiar issue that runs throughout the text—the gains and losses of being part of two cultures. Encourage students to use examples from the other readings to support their points.

HECTOR CALDERON
Reinventing the Border (p. 619)

This essay about Calderón's experiences growing up on the border between California and Mexico could be introduced by referring to the children in the selection from Islas. Islas creates a fictional world from his own knowledge and experience. Calderón talks about his own life in a similar world. For both fictional and nonfictional characters, the border looms as a significant influence on their attitudes and on their lives. Students might want to think carefully about what it means to live on a border and to be part of the cultures on both sides of the border (see question 3). They might want to extend the image of the border to other aspects of life besides the physical one, for example, borders between people, professions, states of mind, and so forth. Question 2 might serve as a focus for a small- or large-group follow-up discussion.

RICHARD RODRIGUEZ
Go North, Young Man (p. 628)

Rodriguez's essay reflects on the nature of the border as a metaphor for other divisions between North American and Latino American ideologies. You might want to discuss it in conjunction with Calderón, Salazar, and Islas.

Students need to understand the history of the relationship between the United States and Mexico to really understand the position of these writers. Question 2 asks them to trace that relationship. Students might want to explore how Texas and California became part of the United States. Question 3 then asks them to think about who is legal and who is not and to reflect on the reasons why so many Mexicans want to move north.

Question 4 raises a recurrent theme in these readings: the problems immigrants have in adapting to a new culture. Students might want to review the Islas selection in this chapter or look at one of the many readings that deal with the problems of assimilation.

AL MARTINEZ
It's a Mad, Mad, Mad, Mad World (p. 635)

This column is a good example of using humor as an effective way to argue a point. However, some students may miss the humor and think that he is being serious—which is why it might be important to discuss the group-activity question that asks students to define satire and decide if the column is satirical. Then students can respond in a journal entry. Your students may wish to send their responses to Mr. Martinez via his email address, al.martinez@latimes.com.

Question 3 builds on the information gathered through working with questions 1 and 2. It asks students to use examples from the reading to show that humor is or is not an effective way of making a point.

Question 4 allows students to try their own hand at writing about a serious topic using humor to make their point.

Connecting (p. 638)

Critical Thinking and Writing

Several of the questions in this set can work in pairs (1 and 7, 3 and 8, and 5 and 9). The first question in each pair, numbers 1, 3, and 5, asks students to answer a question on a specific topic by using information from this chapter. Numbers 7, 8, and 9 ask students to discuss the topic within the text as a whole. Questions 6 and 10 bring up general issues that recur throughout the text.

The Research questions give students an opportunity to find out more about the recent history and concerns of Chicanos.

CHAPTER 9

THE NEW IMMIGRANTS: REVIVING, CHALLENGING, AND REFASHIONING THE AMERICAN DREAM

This chapter, like chapter 3, presents the perspectives of many ethnic groups. Here we have tried to include some representative readings that indicate the richness and diversity of the new immigrants who make up American society. We believe these individuals echo many of the concerns that faced both the early immigrants we presented in chapter 1 and those who were already in this country at that time. Here we read about the same problems of adjustment, assimilation versus cultural pluralism, pride in heritage, and a general coming to terms with themselves and with multicultural America.

The Beginning exercise asks students to speculate about the recent events in specific countries that might make people want to emigrate. The newspaper should be an easy source for material, or your students could narrow this topic and research students at their school. They could find out from admissions how may foreign students attend their university, where they come from, and so forth. They could interview fellow classmates who are immigrants, foreign students, or the children of immigrants. If possible, they might want to contact the foreign student association or club. This is a good way for them to become aware that immigration to America and coming to America to study is an ongoing process. In addition, hearing the experiences of fellow classmates who are recent immigrants should enrich their understanding of the readings.

From Immigration and Nationality Act of 1980 (p. 647)

We chose to present a section of the Immigration and Naturalization Act that dealt with asylum procedures because recently many groups have entered the United States under its provisions. In other cases, such as those concerning refugees from El Salvador, asylum has been denied. Your students might want to investigate the rationale for the government's decisions.

Question 1 might be used to begin the post-reading discussion. It is designed to get students to think about how they would define the term *refugee* and the difficulties of coming up with a precise definition. They might first want to look up the standard definition or create a definition from the context in the text. Next, they should think of ways they would like to modify that definition. This could be used to focus the follow-up small- or large-group discussion. These discussions could also be followed by a writing assignment based on question 4, which asks students to consider current immigration policy. You can ask them to choose any recent historical event and use that to define their criteria for asylum. Once students have formulated a policy, they could be divided into groups according to the criteria they have set up. After discussion within their groups, they might want to debate this issue. You might want to try a debate in which each member of the group researches the question and then participates in an informal debate.

Question 3 would be especially effective if you used the Beginning exercise in class. It gives students the opportunity to internalize the concept of asylum, something that most of them only experience through the media.

CARLOS BULOSAN
My Education (p. 649)

Here Bulosan shows how changes in the American political climate affected his process of self-education. For students to understand the essay, they need to become aware of conditions in America during the Great Depression of the 1930s. You may want to begin by having students work individually or in a group and research those conditions.

Bulosan came to America with many expectations that students need to articulate before they can complete the journal assignment, which asks them to explain why he was disappointed in what he found in America. This will serve as pre-writing for question 3, which asks students to explain his despair and to explore how his faith was restored.

Question 4 examines Bulosan's view of the changing role of the artist as social conditions in America changed. Students might want to discuss the role of artist today and the role of government support for the arts. You might want to show the film *Cradle Will Rock,* which recreates the period of the 1930s and the Federal Theatre Project.

OSCAR HIJUELOS
Visitors, 1965 (p. 654)

This reading also details the experiences of political refugees. In it, the author compares the situation of a family who immigrated in the 1940s with one who immigrates in the 1960s. He reviews the recent history of Cuba and explains why support for Fidel Castro among some Cubans and émigrés declined. He also explores one of the recurring themes in this text, the identity crisis experienced by the bicultural children of immigrants.

You might want to engage students in a pre-reading discussion by asking them what they know about Cuba and its history. If they know very little, they can anticipate having many of their questions answered by the reading. However, you may have Cuban students in the class who can serve as experts and who may be willing to share their own and their family's experiences.

Discussing current immigration and current political situations may create controversy in class. Students, for example, may support one regime or another or may not understand the political situation in a particular country. Most likely, you will be reading this section late in the quarter or semester and by then students should feel that they are part of a community, Those community standards of behavior should include listening to everyone and keeping discussions away from personal attacks. As we mentioned earlier, if things deteriorate in your classroom, you might try to get students to write about what happened and then to discuss it in class. Understanding the dynamics of a situation or why they or someone else is defensive often helps resolve differences.

Question 4 could be used to structure small- or large-group follow-up discussion. Students might discuss whether they sympathize with Mercedes's anger. Alternately, they may wish to discuss Question 2 and explore the political situation in more depth.

If you choose to look at the identity problems encountered by the children of immigrants, you can focus your post-reading discussion on question 3, which replays the recurrent conflict experienced in Okada's *No-no Boy* in Chapter 7, among others. Hector's feelings about Cuba may also be compared to Marisol's in the selection from Cofer's *The Line of the Sun* in chapter 6.

VAN B. LUU
The Hardships of Escape for Vietnamese Women (p. 668)

We chose this reading because, as the author states, at the present time only a limited amount of research is being done on Vietnamese refugee women. This is one of the few published pieces about their situations. In addition, we liked the fact that the research methodology was the personal interview. Interviewing is a method that students can use to conduct primary research. This article serves as a useful model for them. Question 4 asks them to conduct and write up their own interview of a recent immigrant.

Before tackling the reading, students can write at home or in class about their own strategies for handling stress (question 1). This can initiate a discussion of the way in which behavior is shaped by culture as well as personality. Discussion can involve cultural standards, how they develop, and how they are maintained. Students might want to list some of the behaviors dictated by their culture. If you are going to have them write the essay for question 3, you might want them to consider how various cultures define gender roles and assign appropriate behaviors to each.

This reading illustrates the difficulties and dangers that still face immigrants who are forced to flee their homelands. It also shows the desperation that these Vietnamese must have felt to risk this dangerous voyage. An alternate pre-reading activity might have students review the hardships some of the early immigrants faced during their voyages to America.

If students are particularly interested in the Vietnamese, as a post-reading activity they might want to divide into groups and each research one of the issues in question 1. Then they can share their research with the entire class. Vietnamese students in the class can serve as resources. If you prefer a more personal post-reading activity, question 4 could be used as a follow-up, ten-minute in-class writing assignment.

JOSE ALEJANDRO ROMERO
Sumpul (p. 679)

This poem, written by Salvadorean émigré Romero, tells of the massacre at Sumpul in 1980 in which six hundred Salvadoreans lost their lives. Students need to read the headnote to understand the historical context of the poem and may want to know the following additional details about political events in El Salvador that took place within a single year, from May 1979 to May 1980. These events forced the poet and many others into exile. Twenty-five protesters were massacred in front of the Cathedral of San Salvador (May 8, 1979), twenty-five demonstrators were massacred in front of the Venezuelan embassy (May 17, 1980), and Archbishop Oscar Romero was murdered in his church (March 24, 1980). All of these horrors were part of a cycle of disappearances and deaths that came to be almost routine.

As a post-reading discussion, you may want to focus on the effects of such horror on the survivors and the people who were able to escape. Students might want to compare their possible reactions—guilt at surviving, fear, anger, hatred, desire for escape, and revenge—with Miss Sasagawara or the survivors Takaki writes about in chapter 7.

Even without additional information, the poem is a powerful evocation of the horrors of conflict. Students might want to read it aloud and discuss its effect on listeners. After reading, you may want to have students use questions 1 or 2 as the basis for a ten-minute in-class writing assignment.

Question 3 invites students to write a poem about their own experience. They might want to discuss the therapeutic effect of writing about an event that is deeply disturbing. Do they think this is the author's purpose? A discussion of the author's purposes in writing a political poem could be the focus of the post-reading discussion. Again, he can be compared to the Japanese Americans and the Gold Mountain poets in Chapter 4.

BHARATI MUKHERJEE
Visitors (p. 681)

One of the interesting aspects of this selection, and one of the reasons we included it, is the atypical portrayal of immigrants. Unfortunately, immigrants are often stereotyped as poor and uneducated people who come to America because they can't make a successful life for themselves in their home country. The immigrants in this story, however, are wealthy, educated, and successful. We thought it was important for students to understand that immigrants are not all alike, nor are they all poor and needy. Students might want to discuss the circumstances of the characters in this story and compare them to other new immigrants depicted in the chapter. Question 4 asks them to write a formal essay on this topic.

The problems for Vinita, the main character, do not involve problems of sustenance and survival but rather concern issues that confront all people placed in unfamiliar situations: resolving conflict between changed circumstances and expectations. Question 2 asks students to highlight some of the expectations of the new society in which she finds herself and compare them to the expectations of her native culture. Question 3 then asks students to use what they have discovered to help them write a continuation of the story. Understanding Vinita's conflict and situation should help them speculate and support their speculations about her future.

CATHY SONG
Easter: Wahiawa, 1959 (p. 691)

We believe poetry works well when it is read aloud in class. Then students can hear the rhythms the author created. Question 2 directs students to read the poem and analyze the effect of hearing it aloud. Questions 1 invites students to write their own poems or short stories. Working on their own poems may help students understand the difficulties of writing an effective poem. This activity could help them write the essay assignments in questions 3 and 4.

NAOMI SHIHAB NYE
White Coals, A Broken Clock, *and* Speaking Arabic (p. 694)

These three selections can be treated as a whole. They speak of the difficulties of returning home, of having a dual cultural heritage, and of passing a cultural heritage on to one's children. Questions 1, 3, and 4 focus on these issues. However, you may wish to begin with question 2 if your class needs help filling in what the author suggests. Question 2 asks students to consider the form as well as the content of the readings and leads them to articulate much of what is implied in the selections. Working with question 2 would help students understand the readings before trying to work on the essay questions. Question 1 would also serve as a useful pre-reading exercise or might be a good place to begin a post-reading discussion. Students might be very anxious to share their personal experiences. Many may be torn by the same dilemmas the narrators face in these pieces.

Another possibility for a pre-reading discussion is beginning with the question of whether one can go home again. Students might bring up problems they may have encountered in going home during college breaks. How does the old neighborhood seem? Can they still fit in? How do they feel in their new environment?

PETER H. SCHUCK
Border Crossing (p. 697)

Schuck's essay is very complete survey of United States Immigration Law. Students can use it as the basis for the group assignment in question 2. Questions 3 and 4 ask students to think in depth about the laws and what they reflect about public opinion. Students might need to define the stew, salad, and mosaic images before they begin writing. Question 4 asks students to reflect on Schuck's conclusions and to use their own experience and knowledge to agree or disagree with him.

The journal entry is a variation on a theme that runs throughout this text: assimilation versus accommodation. This entry, however, asks students to put themselves in the shoes of a new immigrant and imagine actual strategies and behaviors that they will engage in to further either assimilation or accommodation.

Connecting (p. 703)

Critical Thinking and Writing

Most of the questions in this section ask students to draw conclusions about the immigration experience. They are often expected to compare or cite examples from other parts of the text. At this point in the semester or quarter, students should have read enough of the other readings to be able easily to find those examples. Questions 1 and 4 suggest comparisons between readings within the chapter. Questions 6 through 9 ask students to discuss specific issues raised in this chapter in reference to information gained in reading other chapters. Questions 2, 3, and 5 ask students to discuss broad issues that recur throughout the readings.

The Research topics require outside information. They primarily focus on issues of public policy.

For general suggestions about ways to use the questions, see the Connecting section in Part 1 of this manual.

PART III

THEMATIC TABLE OF CONTENTS

We chose to organize the readings in this text by historical theme because we believe that understanding the context enhances students' appreciation of both the works and the cultures represented. That is not to say, however, that these readings should be restricted to the periods in which they were written. In fact, throughout the text and this manual we have attempted to point up significant themes that recur across cultures and across time.

If you prefer to organize your class thematically, you may find the following thematic table of contents helpful. Needless to say, not every reading has been assigned to a category, and some have been included in several categories. You also might have ideas that you would like to pursue that haven't been considered here. Please bear in mind that this list is meant only to suggest options, not to restrict interpretation.

American Dream

Adams *The Epic of America*
Colón *Kipling and I*
Flynn from *I Speak My Own Piece*
Fukuyama *Immigrants and Family Values*
The Gold Mountain Poems
Kingston *The Grandfather of the Sierra Nevada Mountains*
Krupat *For Multiculturalism*
Lazarus *The New Colossus*
Panunzio *In the American Storm*
Schuck *Border Crossing*
Yezierska *The Fat of the Land*

Arriving in America

Hijuelos *Visitors, 1965*
Hoffman *Lost in Translation*
Kingston *The Grandfather of the Sierra Nevada Mountains*
Luu *The Hardships of Escape for Vietnamese Women*
Panunzio *In the American Storm*
Sui Sin Far *In the Land of the Free*
Young Yu *The World of Our Grandmothers*

Assimilation

Discrimination

Education

Generations

Language

Living Conditions

Looking to the Homeland

Traditions

Brodeur   *The Meaning of the Hunt*
Cofer   from *The Line of the Sun*
Large   *Concerning a Whale*
Welch   *Plea to Those Who Matter*
Yezierska   *The Fat of the Land*

Women

Allen   *Pocahontas to Her English Husband, John Rolfe*
Cisneros   *Woman Hollering Creek*
Sui Sin Far   *In the Land of the Free*
Mukherjee   *Visitors*
Rivera   *Christmas Eve/La Noche Buena*
Rölvaag   *Facing the Great Desolation*
Seller   *Beyond the Stereotype: A New Look at the Immigrant Woman, 1880–1924*
Silko   *Lullaby*
Luu   *The Hardships of Escape for Vietnamese Women*
Yezierska   *The Fat of the Land*
Young Yu   *The World of Our Grandmothers*

Working Conditions

Chávez   *The Organizer's Tale*
Colón   *Kipling and I*
Flynn   from *I Speak My Own Piece*
Kingston   *The Grandfather of the Sierra Nevada Mountains*
Panunzio   *In the American Storm*

PART IV
SUGGESTED FILMS

In assembling this list of films, we chose only those productions that we felt would complement the historical information and general themes in the text. As a result, we were able to locate more films for some chapters than others. Remember, however, that new films are constantly being released and an occasional glance through film source guides can keep you informed of new materials. We found the following guides to be informative, and you may wish to refer to them for additional information: *Educational Film and Video Locator,* R. R. Bowker; *Films and Video for History and Politics,* Penn State Audio-Visual Services; *Native Americans on Film and Video,* Museum of the American Indian/Heye Foundation; and *The Video Source Book,* Gale Research Inc.

At the end of each entry, we have listed the distributor. An index of these distributors and their addresses is given at the end of the film suggestion list.

No films for Chapter 1.

Chapter 2 American Indians

Ancient Spirit, Living Word: The Oral Tradition

This film examines American Indian storytelling.

58 min./color
DIST: Native American Public Broadcasting Consortium

The Forgotten American

The story of the economic, social, and spiritual plight of American Indians.

25 min./color
DIST: CARSL

Images of Indians

A five-part series that traces the stereotypical Hollywood treatment of American Indians through the years.

30 min./color
DIST: UINDIANS; Video Tech

Indian Self-Rule: A Problem of History

Presents a historical outline of federal American Indian policy, focusing on the question of tribal sovereignty.

58 min./color
DIST: DER

Voices of Native Americans

By documenting two American Indian conferences, this film looks at different approaches American Indian leaders are taking to solve current problems.

58 min./color
DIST TWNEWS

Chapter 3 Early Immigrants

America: 9—The Huddled Masses

Alistair Cooke describes immigration to the United States at the end of the nineteenth century.

52 min./color
DIST. AMB

The Immigrant Experience: The Long, Long Journey

Focuses on the problems and dreams of newly landed immigrants in America by dramatizing the struggle of a twelve-year-old Polish immigrant and his family to survive after their arrival in 1907.

28 min./color
DIST LCA

A Storm of Strangers: Jewish-Americans

Photographs of New York's Lower East Side are used to illustrate the story of Jewish immigration to America around the year 1910.

27 min./b&w.
DIST: FI

Chapter 4 Early Chinese Americans

The Chinese-Americans: The Early Immigrants

This film presents the history and contributions of the first Chinese who immigrated to America.

20 min./color
DIST: HFC

The Golden Mountain on Mott Street

Examines the problems encountered by Chinese immigrants to the United States.

38 min./color
DIST: WCBS

A Storm of Strangers: Jung Sai, Chinese-American

A Chinese American journalist traces her heritage by interviewing Chinese of all ages about the early immigrant experience, including building the transcontinental railway, working in the mines, and establishing Chinatowns.

29 min./color
DIST: FI

Chapter 5 African Americans

Civil Rights Movement: The North

Looks at job discrimination, attempted housing integration, and the tense atmosphere of race relations in northern U.S. cities.

22 min./b&w
DIST. FI

Civil Rights Movement: The South

Surveys civil rights movements in the areas of education, public accommodations, and voting rights.

28 min./b&w
DIST FI

Daughters of the Black Revolution

Daughters of slain civil rights leaders Martin Luther King Jr., Medgar Evers, and Malcolm X talk with Phil Donahue.

28 min./color
DIST: FFHS

Do the Right Thing

Portrays the racial tensions surrounding a white-owned pizzeria in the Bedford-Stuyvesant section of Brooklyn on the hottest day of the summer, and the violence that eventually erupts.

95 min./color
DIST: MCA Home Video

El-Hajj Malik El-Shabazz: Malcolm X

Profiles the life of Malcolm X, focusing on the ideas and personal qualities that made him an important leader of the civil rights movement in America in the 1960s.

55 min./b&w
DIST: CRM

Eyes on the Prize

A comprehensive six-part series on the history of the American civil rights movement from World War II to the present.

60 min./color
DIST: PBS Video

Now Is the Time

Recounts the history of African Americans through film clips and dramatic readings, contrasting myths about the "good Negro" of the old minstrel shows with scenes of police beatings and sit-ins in the 1960s.

36 min./b&w
DIST: CARSL

Chapter 6 Puerto Ricans

An Island in America

This program examines the cultural, social, and economic life of Puerto Ricans in the United States.

28 min./color
DIST: ADLBB

Puerto Rico: Americans on the Move

This film explores some of the causes and effects of the migration of Puerto Ricans to New York City and other metropolitan centers.

55 min./b&w
DIST: CBS; MCGH

Puerto Rico: Migration

This film examines the migration of Puerto Ricans to the United States mainland and the problems they face in their new homes. Compares Puerto Rican migration with the waves of Europeans who came to America during the late nineteenth and early twentieth centuries.

9 min./color
DIST: STERLED

Chapter 7 Japanese Americans

Family Gathering

Japanese filmmaker Lisa Yasui uses interviews, home movies, historical footage, and stills to present the experiences of her people in the United States. Special focus is given to the repercussions of her grandfather's internment.

30 min.
DIST: NEWDAY

Guilty by Reason of Race

This film focuses on the events that followed the issue of the Japanese Internment Order. Interviews individuals who went through the experience, some of whom subsequently left the United States and others who remained.

52 min./color
DIST: FI

Invisible Citizens—Japanese Americans

How six Japanese Americans' lives were affected by their internment in concentration camps during World War II.

58 min./color
DIST: Downtown Community TV Center

Chapter 8 Chicanos

Harvest of Shame

A documentary study, narrated by Edward R. Murrow, of the degradation and exploitation of millions of migrant workers in the United States.

53 min./b&w
DIST: CRM

Mexican Americans: An Historic Profile

This program looks at the history of the Mexican American from the Spanish conquistadors to the present.

29 min./b&w
DIST: ADLBB

The Migrants, 1980

Examines the conditions under which itinerant farm workers lived and worked in 1980 and looks at what, if anything, changed for these workers in the twenty years since *Harvest of Shame* (see above) was broadcast.

50 min./color
DIST: FI

One River, One Country: The U.S.-Mexico Border

Correspondent Bill Moyers investigates the "third country" that has emerged along the Rio Grande River, where inhabitants share family and economic ties but feel isolated from the cultures of their native lands, Mexico and the United States.

47 min./color
DIST: CARSL

Raymund Paredes on Chicano Literature

Raymund Paredes, a leading specialist in Chicano cultural studies, discusses the roots and current directions of Chicano literature.

30 min./color
DIST: KPBS

Chapter 9 The New Immigrants

Against Wind and Tide: A Cuban Odyssey

This film focuses on the Cuban refugees who came during the Mariel boatlift in 1980 to show the inconsistencies in American immigration policy.

55 min./color
DIST: FML

The Constitution: That Delicate Balance 11—Immigration Reform

Examines the criteria for admitting foreigners into the United States, legal aliens' rights to social services, employers' responsibilities in hiring undocumented persons, and the extent to which illegal aliens have rights.

56 min./color
DIST: INTELL

The Phans of Jersey City

Documentary portrait of a twenty-member Vietnamese refugee family living in the United States showing how the different family members survive.

49 min./color
DIST: FI

Wanting It All—Immigrant's Dream

Looks at a cross section of immigrants in discussing the rise of legal and illegal immigration in the United States.

22 min./color
DIST: NBC; CARSL

Producer/Distributor List

ADLBB
Anti-Defamation League of B'nai B'rith
823 United Nations Plaza
New York, NY 10017

AMB
Ambrose Video Publishing, Inc.
381 Park Ave. South, Suite 1601
New York, NY 10016

CARSL
Carousel Film and Video
260 Fifth Ave.
New York, NY 10001

CBS
Columbia Broadcasting System
383 Madison Ave.
New York, NY 10017

CHUH
Churchill Films
12210 Nebraska Ave.
Los Angeles, CA 90025

CRM
See MCGH.

DER
Documentary Educational Resources
5 Bridge St.
Watertown, MA 02172

Downtown Community TV Center
87 Lafayette St.
New York, NY 10013

FFHS
Films for the Humanities, Inc.
P.O. Box 2053
Princeton, NJ 08540

FI
Films, Inc., Public Media, Inc.
5547 Ravenswood Ave.
Chicago, IL 60640

FML
Filmakers Library, Inc.
124 E. 40th St., Suite 901
New York, NY 10016

HFC
Handel Film Corporation
8730 Sunset Blvd.
Los Angeles, CA 90069

INTELL
Intellimation, Inc.
2040 Alameda Padre Serra
P.O. Box 4069
Santa Barbara, CA 93140

KPBS
San Diego State University
San Diego, CA 92182

LCA
Learning Corporation of America
Dist. by: Simon and Schuster Communications
108 Wilmot Road
Deerfield, IL 60015

MCA
MCA Home Video
70 Universal City Plaza
Universal City, CA 91608

MCGH
CRM Learning
2233 Faraday Ave.
Carlsbad, CA 92008

NAPBC
P.O. Box 83111
Lincoln, NE 68501

NBC
National Broadcasting Company
30 Rockefeller Plaza
New York, NY 10020

NEWDAY
New Day Films
853 Broadway, Suite 1210
New York, NY 10003

PBS
PBS Video
1320 Braddock Place
Alexandria, VA 22314

STERLED
Sterling Educational Films, Inc.
241 E. 34 St.
New York, NY 10016

TWNEWS
Third World Newsreel
160 Fifth Ave., Room 911
New York, NY 10010

UINDIANS
United Indians of All Tribes Foundation
Administrative Office
Discovery Park
Seattle, WA 98104

Video Tech
19346 3rd Ave., NW
Seattle, WA 98177

WCBS
WCBS-TV
524 W. 57 St.
New York, NY 10019

YOURWV
Your World Video, Inc.
80 8th Ave.
Suite 1701
New York, NY 10011